The Pleasures of the Table *Rediscovering Theodora FitzGibbon*

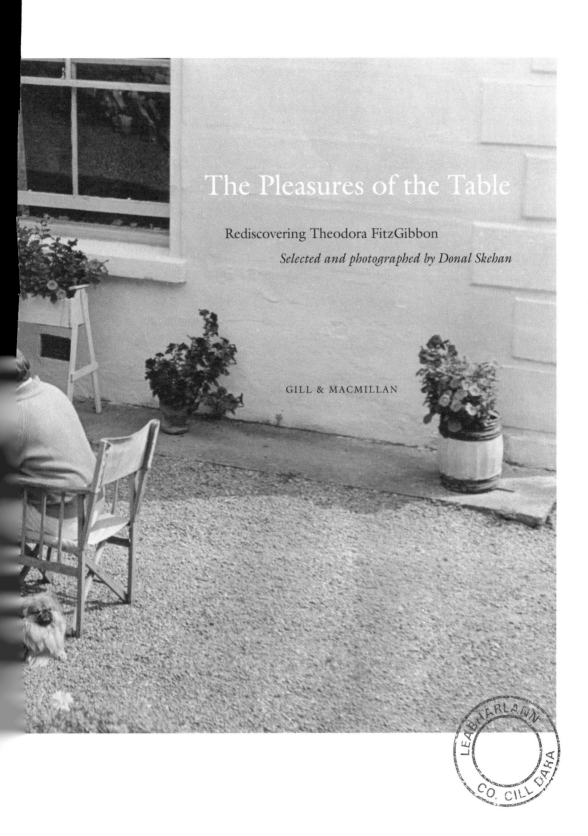

The Pleasures of the Table

Rediscovering Theodora FitzGibbon

Selected and photographed by Donal Skehan

GILL & MACMILLAN

Gill & Macmillan
Hume Avenue, Park West, Dublin 12
www.gillmacmillanbooks.ie

© The Estate of the late Theodora FitzGibbon 2014
© Introduction and food photography, Donal Skehan 2014
978 07171 5967 3

All photographs of Theodora FitzGibbon courtesy of
George Morrison

Index compiled by Eileen O'Neill
Design and print origination by www.grahamthew.com
Printed and bound in Italy by L.E.G.O. SpA

Food styling by Sharon Hearne-Smith
www.blueberrypie.ie, www.twitter.com/SHearneSmith
With thanks to:
Two Wooden Horses, Chapel Road, Greystones, Co. Wicklow.
W: www.twowoodenhorses.com
The Herb Garden, Forde-de-Fyne, Naul, Co. Dublin.
T: 01 841 3907; W: www.theherbgarden.ie

Thanks for the supply of fruit and vegetables from allotments
run by the following businesses:
Country Market, 16 Main Street, Howth, Co. Dublin.
T: 01 832 2033; W: www.countrymarket.ie
Aqua Restaurant, 1 West Pier, Howth, Co. Dublin.
T: 01 832 0690; W: www.aqua.ie

Food props by Sofie Larsson

Kitchen assistants: Louise Dockery, Ajda Mehmet,
Emma Nelson, Nessa Robins, Jette Virdi
Camera assistant: David Corscadden

This book is typeset in 10.5pt Galliard on 12.6pt

The paper used in this book comes from the wood pulp of
managed forests. For every tree felled, at least one tree is
planted, thereby renewing natural resources.

A CIP catalogue record for this book is available
from the British Library.

Note from the publishers: There are some inconsistencies
between measurement conversions in the recipes, but the
ingredients lists are faithful – as far as possible – to the various
books from which they were taken.

5 4 3 2 1

CONTENTS

Breads,
Biscuits and
Cakes

A FOREWORD IN TRIBUTES

George Morrison	As long as I live I shall have the very warmest memories of Theodora. Her spontaneity and originality of personality were quite exceptional. All the time we were together was spent in witty exchanges between one another. She was the absolutely ideal person with whom one could sharpen one's faculties. In fact, there is one solitary occasion when I can recall what seems to me to have been winning an exchange of observations hands down.

It occurred when we were in different rooms. She called out to me some information that I don't now remember and I called back, 'I'm afraid I can't hear you, darling.'

'What do you mean you can't hear me? My voice was trained to carry!'

'Ah, my dear, if only it had been trained to fetch.'

Theodora had, to the fullest extent, that admirable quality which the French call *Coeur* and, besides, she was a marvellous critic, which she applied equally to her own work and to that of others. |
| **Darina Allen, Ballymaloe Cookery School** | Theodora FitzGibbon ought to be remembered as a giant in Irish culinary circles. She was born in London and educated in the UK and France. A beautiful, urbane, scholarly woman, she wrote over thirty books, most of which were about food, with titles as diverse as *Good Housekeeping*, *Good Food for Diabetics*, *Eat Well and Live Longer* and *Making the Most of It*. She also wrote two autobiographies, *With Love: An Autobiography, 1938–1946* and *Love Lies a Loss: An Autobiography, 1946–1959*. However, the books she will be most remembered for are her 'Taste of' series, particularly *A Taste of Ireland* and *A Taste of Scotland*.

For nearly 20 years, for thousands of cooks, me included, her weekly column in *The Irish Times* was essential reading – unmissable. As a novice TV cook and food writer, I met her several times in the 1980s. I respected and admired her writing and scholarship and so was almost embarrassed to find myself replacing her, on the invitation of the then food editor of the Weekend section. I worried that Theodora would be annoyed by this young upstart food writer moving in on her patch. It really mattered to me that she understood how much I respected her and admired her work. |

Domini Kemp

When you mention the name Theodora FitzGibbon to anybody who knows their onions, you are immediately greeted with the fondest recollections of a glamorous, strong and independent woman. As a writer and cook, she had a huge personality and brought a touch of the exotic to everything she did.

Her column in *The Irish Times* – where I now humbly reside – was a force of nature whirling through Irish culinary life and her dishes livened up many tables. Theodora's life was full in ways most of us only dream of, but that isn't to say there weren't hard times too.

However, that immense spirit and ability to entertain gave her a bon viveur sense of the 'table' and placed her in an ideal position to write about food. Her column was loved and adored by so many – and people still talk to me about her legendary Christmas cake. She paved the way for many other writers, including myself, but few could ever match the grace, presence and finesse she brought to every line and page.

Michael Gill, publisher

Her love of life in all its variety translated seamlessly into her passion for food and everything associated with it.

Mary O'Rourke

When I started teaching English many years ago, one of my junior classes seemed to me to be low in the appreciation of *words*. On questioning them, I found that not many of them used the library, not many of them had bought books, and not many of them discussed books among one another. I became very exercised about this and wondered how I could increase their interest in, love of and usage of, words.

At that time every Saturday, Theodora FitzGibbon had a wonderful page in *The Irish Times* which I always devoured – not so much for her cuisine ability and the skills she had to convey, but more for her use of words. Her writing was clear, lucid and often quite quirky in the use of words. She also wrote with great humour and with understanding.

So I hit upon the idea of every Thursday/Friday asking the girls in my class to buy *The Irish Times* on Saturday and then to read her articles. On the Monday following the Saturday, they each brought in their page from *The Irish Times* and we read it, parsed it, talked about it, got out our dictionaries, looked up words and in general marvelled at the skill and ability of Theodora FitzGibbon.

My young students became interested in the nuances of words; very quickly they adapted to using some of the words in different circumstances, and I hope many of them began a life-long love of reading. To me, Theodora FitzGibbon was proof that writing can be lively, vibrant, interesting and attractive.

I can honestly say that by the end of the year I had a class, not just of avid Saturday *Irish Times* readers (hopefully that would come later), but a group of bright young students who would go on to retain an interest in good writing, in good literature, in plentiful usage of good words. Above all, I feel our Theodora FitzGibbon adventure gave rise to curiosity in young people – curiosity about writing, curiosity about words, perhaps even a curiosity about cooking.

Thank you, Theodora, for your help, fadó fadó.

'I do believe that the best food for a country is that which has been continuously tried and tested over the years, which suits the climate and uses the best products of that country.'

INTRODUCTION
Donal Skehan

The history of Irish food is full of enlightened but sometimes forgotten voices. At a time when we are rediscovering the roots of our cuisine, it seems only appropriate that one of those great voices should be celebrated and shared with modern Ireland. Theodora FitzGibbon's knowledge of Irish food and cooking was encyclopedic. Her passion, which can be seen in her extensive catalogue of cookery books, is still inspiring today.

My journey into the world of Theodora FitzGibbon began a couple of years ago when her name came up after a mushroom hunt I was attending. While her name was new to me, those who had read her work and grown up with her recipes extolled her virtues to me as an expert of Irish food who was integral to the very make-up of our cuisine. Before her death in 1991, she had written over 30 cookery titles and served as an *Irish Times* food writer for nearly 20 years. Her popularity was in an Ireland far before my world of social media and food blogs, which means her recipes have stayed solely and exclusively in her printed publications.

After some bargain-hunting online, I managed to order second-hand copies of the vast majority of her books. They arrived at my house in slow succession in varying states of use: dog-eared and splattered with slow-cooked stews and sweet cake batters. Past treasures of kitchens gone by.

The moment I opened my world up to this grand lady of Irish cuisine, she seemed to rush into my life. I made my way through her fascinating two-book autobiography, a hand-me-down from my aunt. I pored over the many newspaper clippings my grandmother had saved over the years from Theodora's highly popular *Irish Times* column. However, the true highlight was discovering her beautiful recipes and recreating them in my kitchen. I served her Rabbit Pie to my grandad and it rekindled memories of his time as a bachelor when rabbit was all he knew how to cook, while her Mutton Pies and Lemon Marshmallow Cake proved a hit with a slightly younger audience and were served to a chorus of approval from my friends.

Classic recipes – like her Christmas cake – had become legendary and well used in homes across Ireland throughout the 1970s and 1980s, cementing her as a voice of knowledge and as an instant portal to reliable recipes. Apart from her knowledge of Irish food, the fact that she travelled widely throughout her life also had a large part to play in the success of her career as a food writer, providing her with foreign ingredients and influences from far-flung places.

In early 2013, just when I had finished reading her autobiography, I was contacted by Gill & Macmillan, Theodora's Irish publishing home. They were working on a project to republish a collection of her recipes. We discussed the idea of presenting her work from a new viewpoint and they asked me to take on the daunting task of selecting recipes from her huge collection and photographing them.

A meeting was set up with Theodora's husband, film-maker and photographic restorer, George Morrison. Naturally the meeting was over lunch. As we settled into Cavistons restaurant in Glasthule, and over George's recommendation of scallops, we discussed Theodora's approach to food as well as their relationship. Most important, however, was George's approval of this 'young man' to work on the project.

George photographed all of the recipes for Theodora's *Irish Times* columns and has an extensive collection of food photographs which he has exhibited. He invited me to visit the home he had shared with Theodora for a viewing of her recipe images and to watch his film *These Stones Remain*. George warned me that a good food photograph should stay true to three key components – form, texture and colour – and told me that his one rule as a food photographer was to make sure that he tried all of the food that passed beneath his camera. A rule I also stick to quite firmly!

A truly magical moment during my journey into the world of Theodora was the discovery of her contribution to an RTÉ radio documentary on the history of the Irish potato, which aired on 18 February 1984. Although I had spent time with her text and recipes, her speaking voice had been silent. Then, all of a sudden, exactly how I had imagined, she was there in the room, booming and proud. She spoke at length about the Irish and our relationship with an ingredient that has come to define our nation.

Her voice was full of authority and expertise, with a no-nonsense approach to modern-day practices. The powerful timbre of her voice stuck with me as we cooked through the recipes I had selected from her vast back catalogue. The mantra 'What would Theodora do?' was used many times as we made decisions on how to plate-up dishes and present the food for camera. It is this voice and the present-day inheritors of Theodora FitzGibbon's great knowledge who continue to inspire me on my journey in food.

The recipes you will find in this book stand as a strong testament to a fine Irish food writer. My hope is that it will give a new generation of cooks the inspiration and wisdom Theodora FitzGibbon has given me.

Donal Skehan
Howth, Dublin
October 2013

SOUPS

'There is nothing quite so warming as a good soup.'

Carrot and Orange Soup

450 g (1 lb) carrots, finely chopped

1 large onion, finely chopped

1.7 litres (3 pints) chicken stock

juice and grated rind of 2 small oranges

pinch ground coriander

salt and pepper

2–3 tablespoons cream or creamy milk

fresh corriander, chopped

200 g (7 oz) butter

brown bread to serve

Put the prepared carrots and onion into a large saucepan and add the stock. Bring to the boil and simmer until the carrots are quite soft. Liquidise and put back into the saucepan, then add the juice of the oranges and the coriander. Heat up and taste for seasoning. Serve garnished with the cream or creamy milk and fresh coriander, along with brown bread spread with butter which has been worked with the finely grated orange rind.

SERVES ABOUT 6

French Onion Soup

Also known as *soupe d'oignon gratinée*, this was an old favourite with the porters of the now dismantled Les Halles Market in Paris.

Heat the oil or butter in a saucepan and add the peeled, sliced onions. Cook gently, stirring frequently until they are golden – on no account let them brown. Stir in the flour and add the pepper and salt. Pour over the stock or Marmite dissolved in hot water (in some ways I prefer this to stock, for it gives a more authentic French flavour), cover and cook gently for about 25 minutes.

Meanwhile, dry the slices of bread in the oven. Pour the hot, unstrained soup into either individual fireproof dishes or one large one, then transfer the slices of bread to the soup, sprinkling thickly with grated cheese. In some country areas a tablespoon of cream is also poured over, but it rather changes the fine, clear flavour. Before serving put under a hot grill for a few minutes to brown the cheese.

SERVES 4–6

4 large onions, peeled and sliced

2 tablespoons flour

2 tablespoons oil or butter

2.4 litres (4 pints) beef stock (dissolved stock cubes or 2 teaspoons Marmite, dissolved)

salt and pepper

thick slices of stale French or Vienna loaves

110 g (4 oz) grated cheese

Nettle Soup

110 g (4 oz) butter

1 large leek or 2 medium-sized leeks, chopped

4 cups nettle tops, chopped

450 g (1 lb) potatoes, sliced

1 litre (1 ¾ pints) chicken stock

salt and freshly ground pepper

150 ml (¼ pint) cream

chive flowers to garnish

This soup is a great favourite in the spring when the nettles are young. Nettles are full of minerals and vitamins which purify the blood. In the country nettle tea was also drunk, made by pouring boiling water over chopped nettles, boiling for about 15 minutes, then straining and adding milk and sugar. This was often given to children who had measles. It is said to have been a favourite of St Columcille.

Nettle soup is still served in some hotels in Ireland; this recipe is from Declan Ryan, who was chef-proprietor of the much-starred Arbutus Lodge, Cork, sadly no longer in existence.

Use gloves and a scissors when cutting the nettles. Do not gather them from sprayed verges or after the end of May as they will be too tough.

Heat the butter until foaming. Add the chopped leek and the nettle tops and cook until they look glossy. Stir in the potatoes, then add the stock. Simmer gently for 30–35 minutes. Sieve or liquidise the soup, return to the heat, season to taste and add the cream. Garnish with chive flowers and serve hot.

SERVES 6

Leek and Oatmeal Soup

4–6 large leeks, ends trimmed

2 tablespoons butter

1.5 litres (2 ½ pints) half
milk and half chicken stock

2 rounded tablespoons
oatmeal flakes

salt and freshly ground pepper

2 tablespoons parsley, chopped

150 ml (¼ pint) cream
to garnish

This is a traditional soup. It is not only delicious and easy to make but also full of fibre!

Wash the leeks well to remove grit; trim, but leave most of the fresher green parts, then chop into chunks of about 2.5 cm (1 in) and wash again if needed. Put the butter with the milk and stock in a large saucepan over medium heat. When it boils, add the oatmeal and boil for 5 minutes, then add the leeks and season well. Cover and simmer gently for about 30 minutes. Then add half the parsley and cook for 5 minutes. Serve in heated bowls with a little cream in each and some parsley sprinkled over.

SERVES ABOUT 6

VARIATION: *If liked, you can make some bacon croûtons by cooking some streaky rashers until crisp, then crush and sprinkle over.*

Pea Soup

An enchanting recipe from Sara Power's manuscript book, 1746, is for 'Pease Soop':

Boyl 2 quarts of pease, in six quarts of water till tender then take out some of the clear liquor, and strain the pease clean from the hasks, then put in your pease, and liquor together, and boyl them well, take what butter you think fit, and boyl it up in a pan, then put in some onions cut Small, some Sorrell, Sollory, and Spinage cut them pritty large and let them boyl for a quarter of an hour in the butter. Take some flower and bland it and mix it with a little of the liquor, or in the butter which you will then mix all with your soop, and put in salt, pepper, cloves and other spices as you please, with some sweet cream mix'd with all. Then take french rouls and crisp them before please, and lay them in the middle of the dish, and power in your soop and serve it hot, with a little lemon peel grated round the brim of the Dish.

I would say that generally peas are the most popular vegetable in Ireland: fresh, frozen and dried. The large whole dried peas are usually the variety called 'marrowfat' and maybe it was the name that attracted a lot of hungry people. They are large and mealy and need an overnight's soaking before they can be cooked, although nowadays they are processed and 2 hours' soaking is often enough. They are still used, especially with corned pork or beef, and when mashed are known as 'mushy' peas. They make a good winter soup, as do also the split version of the dried peas which come in both a green and a yellow colour. I have found no difference in the taste, but perhaps the green looks more appetising. The perfect stock to use with dried peas is that left from boiling bacon or ham or, if it is not too salty, corned beef or pork.

De-rind the bacon and cut into dice, and put into a large saucepan with the bacon fat or oil. Soften, then add the chopped onion and soften. Add the soaked peas, bay leaf, thyme, mint and stock. Bring to the boil, cover and simmer for about 2 hours or until the peas are a purée. Add the Worcestershire sauce and taste for seasoning. Lift out the herbs and stir the soup well. If too thick add some milk or cream and bring back nearly to boiling point. Garnish with chopped parsley and, if liked, some crumbled bacon.

SERVES 6–8

4 streaky rashers of bacon or a ham bone

1 tablespoon bacon fat or oil

1 large onion, chopped

450 g (1 lb) dried split peas, soaked for at least 3 hours, or whole ones soaked overnight

2 teaspoons Worcestershire sauce

salt and pepper

milk or cream, optional

chopped parsley to garnish

1 bay leaf

1 sprig thyme

1 sprig mint

2 ½ litres (4 ½ pints) stock

Chicken Farmhouse Soup

1 boiling fowl, about 1 ½ kg
(3 ¼ lb), cut into joints or
equivalent chicken portions

salt

bouquet garni of parsley,
thyme and tarragon

1 medium-sized onion, sliced

1 medium-sized carrot, sliced

1 small blade mace

small pinch mixed spice

2 stalks celery, chopped

1 bay leaf

110 g (4 oz) bacon or ham,
coarsely chopped

50 g (2 oz) oatmeal or 2
large egg yolks, beaten,
with 3 tablespoons cream

pepper

This soup was made in the days when boiling fowls were easy to get and full of flavour. It can be a hearty meal or is equally well served as a fine-flavoured starter for a dinner party.

Wipe the chicken over and remove any lumps of fat from its inside. Rub with salt and put the bouquet garni inside. Put into a large saucepan with about 2 ¼ litres (4 pints) water. Bring to the boil, then simmer for half an hour after skimming off any scum. Add the onion, carrot, mace, mixed spice, celery, bay leaf and bacon or ham. Bring back to the boil, lower the heat and simmer for about 2 hours or until the chicken is tender. If including the oatmeal, add after 1 hour and stir well.

Take out the chicken portions, and bone, skin and chop into neat pieces. If not including the oatmeal, strain the soup before returning the chicken pieces to it and add the beaten egg and cream mixture. Otherwise simply return the chicken pieces to the soup. Heat almost to boiling point, adding pepper and salt to taste. Serve in large soup plates with a good portion of chicken in each.

SERVES AT LEAST 6

Bacon Broth

The pig was probably the first domesticated animal in Ireland. This soup is very like the French *pot-au-feu* in that the soup was often drunk first and then the meat served as a second course with the vegetables.

Other meats such as mutton, beef, lamb or game, such as rabbit, can also be used, either in place of the bacon or with it. A mixture of rabbit and bacon is very good. It can also be made with stock from boiled bacon, or with a meaty ham bone, rather than with the bacon, in which case salt may need to be added to taste. This makes a very substantial soup-stew – delicious on a cold day.

Drain the soaked bacon and put into a large saucepan with water to cover. Bring to the boil and take off any scum, then add the pearl barley and the lentils. Bring to the boil and simmer for 15 minutes. Add the onions, carrots, parsnips, swede, pepper, thyme, bay leaf and parsley. Bring to the boil, lower heat and simmer gently for a further 15 minutes. Add the potatoes and the cabbage, and bring to the boil again. Simmer until they are tender but not mushy, perhaps another 15 minutes. By this time the barley, lentils and piece of bacon should be cooked; if not, cook a little longer. Finally, add the chopped leek and chopped parsley, and cook for about 5 minutes more or until the leek is just tender.

Remove the bacon and take off the skin. If eating with the soup, cut into either small cubes or thin slices, put back into the pot and serve a little in each soup plate. If the soup is to be eaten first, slice the meat on a serving dish, garnish (perhaps with some freshly cooked vegetables) and keep warm while the soup is served.

SERVES 4–6

900 g (2 lb) shoulder or collar bacon, soaked overnight
2 tablespoons pearl barley
2 tablespoons lentils
2 medium-sized onions, sliced
4–6 medium-sized carrots, sliced
2 medium-sized parsnips, sliced
½ medium-sized swede, sliced
pepper
1 sprig thyme
1 bay leaf
1 sprig parsley
450 g (1 lb) potatoes, peeled and sliced
1 small cabbage, quartered
1 leek, chopped
2 tablespoons parsley, chopped

Irish Farmhouse Soup (Mutton Broth)

From about 1846 rice was used a lot in Irish cooking. This type of soup – made with cheaper cuts of meat, vegetables and a cereal – exists in country kitchens all over the Western world. Instead of using mutton, this soup can be made with stewing beef, a little ham or bacon, or simply some meaty bones, and whatever vegetables are available.

Bone the meat and trim of fat and gristle, then cut into small pieces. Put the bones on to cook in enough water to cover, allowing them to simmer gently while you prepare the vegetables. Strain the bones, reserving the stock. Put the meat into a large saucepan with the peas (if using dried ones) and the pearl barley (if using). Add about 2 ¼ litres (4 pints) of the bone stock made up with water. Add salt, bring to the boil, then simmer, skimming if necessary. Cover and cook for about half an hour, then add all the cut-up vegetables and continue simmering for another half an hour. If using, add the fresh peas and rice and cook for another 10–15 minutes. Serve with a lot of chopped parsley.

SERVES 8–10

700 g (1 ½ lb) neck of mutton, or equivalent meat and bone

1 tablespoon dried split peas, soaked, or 110 g (4 oz) fresh peas

2 tablespoons pearl barley or rice

salt

1 large onion, chopped

3 medium-sized carrots, cut up

1–2 celery stalks

1 large leek, cleaned well and cut up

1–2 turnips, thinly sliced

parsley, chopped

Cockle Soup

'Cockles and mussels alive, alive oh!'

about 50 cockles

2 heaped tablespoons butter

2 heaped tablespoons flour

600 ml (1 pint) creamy milk

1 cup celery, chopped

2 tablespoons parsley, chopped

salt and pepper

150 ml (¼ pint) cream

These members of the *Cardium* family are first cousins of the clam and are very numerous on shores, particularly in the west of Ireland. In Kerry they are known as 'carpetshell' and 'kirkeen' and are easy to distinguish as they have a smooth surface with a slight ridge running vertically over the shell. Nowadays many are exported to Europe.

In the old days when white flour was not only a luxury but also a rarity, this soup would have been thickened with a handful of wheaten flour or oatmeal, either of which would give a lovely nutty flavour.

Scrub and wash the cockles very well and discard any that are open. Put into a large saucepan with enough salted water (preferably using sea salt) to barely cover. Bring to the boil, shaking the pan occasionally. Cook until the shells are open, then remove at once and let cool until you can handle them. Take the cockles from their shells and strain the liquid. Heat the butter and, when foaming, add the flour and cook for 1 minute, then gradually add the strained cockle juice and the milk, stirring until smoothly blended. Add the chopped celery and cook for 5 minutes, then add the chopped parsley and taste for seasoning. Bring to the boil for a few minutes. Finally, put back the cockles and heat gently. Add the cream either to the saucepan or to the individual soup bowls.

SERVES 4–6

Shrimp Bisque

350 g (12 oz) shrimps or prawns

2 tablespoons butter

2 stalks celery, finely chopped

110 g (4 oz) mushrooms, sliced

1 rounded tablespoon flour

300 ml (½ pint) milk

300 ml (½ pint) cream

salt and pepper

4–5 tablespoons dry sherry or dry white wine

2 egg yolks, beaten, with a spoonful of cream, optional

cayenne pepper

This is a grander version of the ordinary shellfish soup based on similar soups served in eighteenth-century France. The small shrimp (*Crangon crangon*) was originally used, but the larger prawn or Dublin Bay prawn (*Nephrops norvegicus*) can also be used if chopped smaller. Frozen shrimps or prawns can also be used for this.

Shell the shrimps or prawns and put the shells in a saucepan with 600 ml (1 pint) water. Simmer for about half an hour, then strain the stock. Melt the butter in a saucepan and, when foaming, put in the celery. When it is just becoming opaque, add the mushrooms and soften them. Add the flour, mix well and cook for 1 minute, stirring. Add the stock (or water), bring to the boil and simmer for about 15 minutes. Either sieve or liquidise, then put into a clean pan. Add the shrimps or prawns and the milk and cream, and season to taste. Bring to the boil and simmer for 5 minutes. Add the sherry or wine and reheat. If a richer soup is liked, beat the yolks of 2 eggs with a spoonful of cream and add gradually, but do not let it boil after this addition. Garnish with a little cayenne pepper.

SERVES 4

Gazpacho

Gazpacho is an iced Portuguese and Spanish soup. Traditionally all ingredients were pounded in a mortar, but nowadays a blender is used. However, in the absence of a blender, use a Mouli vegetable mill.

Without a blender, put all the peeled vegetables through the mill, then add the breadcrumbs. Add the oil, drop by drop, until it becomes a thick paste, then slowly add the wine vinegar and the iced water. Serve cold, in soup-plates with an ice cube in the centre of each portion. Fried croûtons are served separately but are not essential.

If using a blender, combine all ingredients (except the breadcrumbs and ice cubes) in the container. Cover and blend at high speed for about 4 seconds only, or until the vegetables are coarsely chopped but not pulverised. Serve chilled with an ice cube in the centre as above.

SERVES 6

1 small peeled cucumber

1 small peeled onion

2 tablespoons white breadcrumbs (not needed if using a blender)

2 cloves peeled garlic

salt and pepper

4 large, ripe peeled tomatoes

1 small peeled green pepper

2 tablespoons wine vinegar

2 tablespoons olive oil

½ cup iced water and ice cubes

croûtons of fried bread to garnish

POULTRY AND GAME

'A boiled chicken is a useful thing to have
to hand, and very good for the impromptu
picnic as well as for making other more
elaborate dishes from.'

Pot-roasted Chicken with Apples

1 chicken, about 2 kg (4 ½ lb)

450 g (1 lb) cooking apples, peeled, cored and thinly sliced

pinch each ground cloves, ground ginger and dried sage

700 g (1 ½ lb) sausage meat

1 large onion, sliced

juice and grated peel of 1 lemon

2 teaspoons sugar or to taste

½ large onion, chopped

2 tablespoons oil

flour for sprinkling

600 ml (1 pint) cider or apple juice

salt and pepper

freshly cooked carrots and peas to garnish, optional

For cooking a mature bird, this is a good method for the autumn when windfall apples are available.

Wipe the chicken over and remove the lumps of fat from the inside. Combine half the sausage meat with the onion slices and about three quarters of the apple slices. Add the spices, lemon peel and sugar, and mix well. Stuff the bird with the mixture and secure well. Heat the oil and quickly brown the chicken all over, then sprinkle with flour and cook for another minute or two, turning it in the fat. Transfer to a casserole. Roll the rest of the sausage meat into little balls about the size of large walnuts and sprinkle them with flour. Combine the remainder of the apple slices with the chopped onion, then put around the chicken and arrange the sausage meatballs on top.

Heat the cider or apple juice and pour into the pan. Cover and cook gently on top of the stove or in a low oven at 150°C/300°F/gas mark 2 for 1–1 ½ hours. To serve, lift the bird onto a warmed serving dish, arrange the balls around it and spoon a little of the pan juices over the chicken: serve the remainder separately, or if a thicker sauce is required boil it up on top of the stove to reduce it slightly. The chicken looks attractive garnished with young buttered carrots and peas.

SERVES 6

Roman Chicken

1 roasting chicken, jointed

seasoned flour

4 tablespoons oil

450 g (1 lb) mixed red and green peppers

150 g (5 oz) canned tomatoes

1 garlic clove, chopped

pinch rosemary, chopped

600 ml (1 pint) chicken stock (use beef for the beef dish)

salt and freshly ground pepper

This good and colourful Roman dish can also be made with stewing beef, using about 900 g (2 lb) and increasing the cooking time by 30 minutes.

Wipe the chicken joints and take off the skin and any fat, then roll in the seasoned flour. Prepare the peppers by deseeding and cutting into strips. Heat up half the oil in a pan and sauté the peppers, then put into a casserole dish. Add the remaining oil to the pan and quickly sauté the chicken joints until golden all over, then add the herb, garlic, tomatoes and stock, and season to taste. Boil up, then pour over the peppers and mix very well. Cover and cook in a moderate oven at 180°C/350°F/gas mark 4 for about 1 ½ hours, checking halfway through cooking time and giving it a stir. Test for tenderness before removing from the oven.

SERVES 4–6

Chicken Lahori

A very colourful dish from India, which is not at all hot but extremely full of flavour. It should marinade in its topping for about an hour before cooking and should not be cooked ahead of time. (See also Plaice Lahori, page 86.)

This can also be made with chicken joints and the marinade equally divided. It is best to buy either breast or thigh joints for this method, but keep cooking time to 90 minutes.

Mix all the marinade ingredients on a deep plate, pounding well, then add the olive oil and mix in thoroughly. Put the chicken in the dish and rub this marinade all over, especially over the breast and legs. Cover and leave to marinade, turning at least once. It can stay longer in the marinade if convenient. Line a baking tin with foil, put the chicken into the middle, then the marinade all over the breast and legs. Secure foil loosely at the top.

Preheat oven to 200°C/400°F/gas mark 6 and put the bird in for half an hour, then lower heat to 180°C/350°F/gas mark 4 and continue cooking for another hour. Take out and roll back foil, then put back in oven so that the top and legs can brown – about 20 minutes is usually enough, but check that the Lahori marinade is not drying up. Put onto a warm serving dish with the pan juices and serve with freshly boiled rice and wedges of lemon.

SERVES 4–6

1 chicken

MARINADE

2 tablespoons onion, finely minced

juice of 1 lemon

¼ teaspoon ground coriander, or fresh leaves, chopped

pinch minced or powdered garlic

pinch turmeric

1 cm (½ in) stem chopped green ginger or drained ginger in syrup

pulp of 2 large ripe tomatoes (canned and drained can be used)

salt and pepper

about 2 tablespoons olive oil

Parmesan Oven-fried Chicken

50 g (2 oz) butter

4 large chicken portions

1 heaped tablespoon flour

2 tablespoons grated
Parmesan cheese

good pinch oregano or rosemary

salt and pepper

SAUCE

1 rounded tablespoon seasoned
flour

150 ml (¼ pint) chicken stock

150 ml (¼ pint) single cream

Melt the butter in a shallow roasting tin, then dip the chicken joints (skinned if you prefer) in the butter and lightly coat with the flour and cheese mixed with the herb, pepper and salt. Lay in a single layer in the pan, skin side up. Bake uncovered in a preheated oven at 220°C/425°F/gas mark 7 for 20 minutes, then turn over and cook for a further 10 minutes or until golden and tender.

Lift out the chicken to a warmed dish and keep warm. Put the pan juices on top of the stove and mix in a rounded tablespoon of seasoned flour and cook for 1 minute. Add 150 ml (¼ pint) chicken stock, stirring well, and finally the same amount of thin cream. Boil rapidly for about 2 minutes, stirring well. Pour this around the crispy joints and serve with puréed potatoes and either a green vegetable or a green salad.

SERVES 4–6

Honey-glazed Chicken

Also a good recipe for pork and lamb.

Soften the butter (but do not let it oil) and mix the other ingredients in, then coat the chicken joints with this mixture. Line a baking tin with foil to avoid sticking and roast in a moderate oven at 180°C/350°F/gas mark 4 for about 1 hour.

SERVES 4–6

1.4 kg (3 lb) chicken, cut into joints

110 g (4 oz) butter or margarine

6 tablespoons honey

2 tablespoons light French mustard

2 level teaspoons curry powder

Fifteen Minute Boiled Chicken with Lemon Sauce

1 large chicken, about 1.8–2.3 kg(4–5 lb)

1 lemon, cut in half

herbs of your choice

1 piece ginger, about 2.5 cm (1 in) across

2¼ litres (4 pints) water

1–2 chicken stock cubes

salt and pepper

and most important, 4 silver or silver plated spoons or forks

Large chickens, unless they are capons that is (castrated cocks that are specially fattened for roasting), are extremely good if boiled – this does not mean a limp bird that has been cooking for hours – and served with a parsley sauce. The following method was given to me some years ago by a Chinese cook and to begin with I thought it was an inscrutable Oriental joke. However, having once tried it, I never boil chickens any other way, and the many friends I have told about it feel the same way.

Wash the chicken thoroughly inside and out, then sprinkle salt inside, and rub the outside with the lemon. Boil up 4 pints of water in a large saucepan and add the ginger, stock cubes and herbs. Put the four spoons or forks *inside* the bird, and when the water is boiling add the chicken. Season to taste, put the lid on and boil for 15 minutes. Then turn out the flame, keep the lid tightly on and allow to go cold.

You will have a beautifully cooked chicken all ready to serve cold or to be heated up in any sauce you like. It is something to do with the heat radiating from the silver, but do not ask me to explain it. Damn clever, those Chinese! If you want to serve it cold, remove the skin and coat the chicken with the following lemon sauce.

LEMON SAUCE

2 tablespoons butter or margarine

600 ml (1 pint) chicken stock, warm

2 tablespoons flour

juice of 1 lemon

grated peel of 1 lemon to garnish

about 2 tablespoons parsley to garnish

Melt the butter, stir in the flour and add the warm chicken stock, stirring all the time until it is thick. Add the lemon juice and season to taste. Let it cool slightly, then cover the chicken with this sauce. Sprinkle the grated peel and parsley on top.

SERVES 6–8

Chicken Biryani

Chicken biryani is a dry curry from Pakistan and not unlike a pilaff, for it is a meal on its own and does not require accompaniments. Half-cooked rice is used and any meats; poultry, fish and suchlike can be used. Small amounts can utilise leftovers.

Mix the yoghurt, garlic and all spices together, and marinate the chicken joints in the mixture for about 2 hours. Meanwhile, brown the onions in the butter or oil and mix with the chicken in a casserole; salt and cook in a moderate oven at 180°C/350°F/gas mark 4 until the bird is done – this generally takes about 1 hour. Then take all the meat from the bird and layer it with the rice in the casserole, pouring the sauce over the top. If it seems very dry, add not more than 1 cup of water, put the lid on and heat up in the oven. Serve on a large hot dish and decorate the top with the sliced eggs, cucumber and nuts.

SERVES 6–8

1 large chicken, about 1.8–2.3 kg (4–5 lb), jointed

4 cloves garlic

½ teaspoon powdered turmeric

1 tablespoon garam masala

pinch ground ginger

1 tablespoon ground coriander (*dhaniya*)

450 g (1 lb) long-grain rice (cooked for 10 minutes)

3 large onions, finely sliced

110 g (4 oz) butter or oil

600 ml (1 pint) plain yoghurt

salt and pepper

sliced hard-boiled eggs, peeled and sliced tomatoes, cucumber, and slivered almonds can be used, either all or some, as a garnish before serving

Chicken and Leek Pie

175 g (6 oz) shortcrust
pastry (see page 260)

1 chicken, about 1.8 kg (4 lb),
jointed, chopped and boned

4 slices thick gammon or ham

4 large leeks, well cleaned
and chopped

1 medium-sized onion or
2 shallots, finely sliced

salt and pepper

pinch ground mace or nutmeg

300 ml (½ pint) chicken stock

150 ml (¼ pint) double cream

milk for brushing

This is a delicious pie which forms a soft jelly when cold. It can also be made with rabbit or with a mixture of chicken and rabbit.

Make the pastry and leave to rest in a cold place. Meanwhile, prepare the pie. In a deep 1–1.5-litre (2-pint) pie dish place layers of the chicken, ham, leeks and onion or shallot, adding the mace or nutmeg and seasoning, then repeating the layers until the dish is full. Add the stock, then dampen the edges of the dish before rolling out the pastry to the required size. Place the pastry over the pie, pressing the edges down well, and then crimp with a fork. Make a small hole in the centre, then roll out the scraps of pastry and form a leaf or rosette for the top and place this very lightly over the small hole. Brush the pastry with milk and bake in the centre of the oven at moderate heat, 180°/350°F/gas mark 3, for 25–30 minutes.

Cover the pastry with damp greaseproof paper when partially cooked if the top seems to be getting too brown. Gently heat the cream. Remove the pie from the oven when cooked. Carefully lift off the rosette and pour the cream in through the hole. Put back the rosette and serve.

SERVES 4

Chicken in Orange Sauce

1.6 kg (3 ½ lb) chicken, jointed

SAUCE
2 tablespoons grated orange rind
450 ml (¾ pint) orange juice
50 g (2 oz) brown sugar
2 thinly sliced oranges to garnish
50 g (2 oz) melted margarine
2 teaspoons mild mustard
1 teaspoon salt
1 tablespoon cornflour

This is an Israeli recipe using Jaffa oranges.

If you do not want to use a jointed chicken, then you can split it in half. Then lay it skin side down in a greased roasting pan. Combining well, mix the orange rind, orange juice, sugar, mustard and salt, and pour this mixture over the bird, rubbing well into the flesh. Leave for about 1 hour. Preheat the oven to 220°C/420°F/gas mark 7.

Put the pan into the oven and bake for 45 minutes, basting frequently with the orange juice mixture. After it has been cooking for 30 minutes, turn so that the skin gets brown. Check that it is cooked through, otherwise leave for another 15 minutes. Put onto a warmed dish and keep warm.

Mix the cornflour to a paste with a little cold water. Bring the chicken gravy to a gentle simmer on top of the stove, add the cornflour and stir well. Cook for about 3 minutes, then pour sauce over the chicken and garnish.

SERVES 4–6

VARIATIONS: This same recipe can be used for pork. For lamb, roast for 45 minutes to 1 hour for 1.4 kg (3 lb), then add the orange juice to de-fatted pan juices, followed by the finely shredded rind. Continue cooking and baste every 25 minutes. Grated orange peel and orange juice are very good added to bread and herb stuffings for pork, lamb or chicken, and this orange stuffing is good between 2 pork chops, trimmed of fat, then baked in orange juice for 1–1 ¼ hours.

Djej Matisha Mesla

This is an exciting chicken dish which comes from a great centre of Moorish-Andalusian culture, a place called Tetuan in north Morocco. They use tomatoes in it and there is a sweetish flavour that comes from a dark honey. It is quite delicious and easy to do but should be started the day before in the marinade below – a most lovely dish for a party which can be reheated.

Wipe the chicken and remove any lumps of fat. Put the turmeric, ginger and pepper in a bowl with the crushed garlic and salt, moisten with some oil and mix well. Rub this into the chicken flesh, cover and leave for at least 4 hours or overnight.

Put the chicken with the oil, grated onion and 300 ml (½ pint) water into a casserole, bring to the boil, reduce to a simmer and cook uncovered for 10 minutes. Then add the tomatoes, tomato purée, cinnamon and a little salt. Mix well and cook over a fairly high heat, turning from time to time until the chicken is tender, about 25–30 minutes, ensuring it does not catch. Then when the chicken is cooked, stir in the honey. Turn over a low heat and finally sprinkle with the nuts. Serve with dry boiled rice.

SERVES 4–6

1 chicken, jointed
2 garlic cloves, peeled
salt
pinch each ground turmeric, ginger and black pepper
2 tablespoons oil
1 medium-sized onion, grated
900 g (2 lb) ripe tomatoes, peeled and chopped
1 level tablespoon tomato purée
½ teaspoon ground cinnamon
2 tablespoons thick honey
2 tablespoons almonds or sesame seeds, toasted

Wild Duck with Mustard Sauce

1 duck, weighing at least
1.1–1.4 kg (2 ½–3 lb), or use
2 smaller ducks

salt and pepper

350 g (12 oz) duck's liver

25 g (1 oz) butter

1 medium-sized onion, chopped

150 ml (½ pint) red wine

juice of ½ lemon or orange

grated peel of the lemon or
orange

2 teaspoons Dijon mustard

A mild Dijon mustard should be used rather than a hot kind.

Season the duck inside and out. Prick the skin slightly, put into a tin and roast at 190°C/370°F/gas mark 5 for about 40 minutes. While the duck is cooking, sauté the liver, then mash it up to a paste in the butter. Sauté the onion until soft but not coloured, then add the wine. Boil, then lower heat and simmer, and add the liver paste and the rest of the ingredients. Stir well. Bring up to heat and keep warm. Carve the duck(s) into portions or place whole onto a serving dish and cover with a little of the sauce, serving the rest separately.

SERVES 6–8

Braised Goose with Dumplings

Goose – often boiled or braised – was the usual bird for the festive occasions in Ireland until the twentieth century, for it must be remembered that in the humbler homes there was no oven, just a big turf fire with hooks and jacks and a large black pot (which accounts for the term 'to take pot luck'). There is an old saying in Ireland that if you eat goose on Michaelmas on 29 September, you will have good fortune all the year round.

FROM KNOCKNAGOW *BY CHARLES J. KICKHAM, C. 1870S*
Now this young farmer partook of boiled goose in his own house on an average once a week – that is to say, every Sunday since Michaelmas. And a very savoury dish, too, is goose and dumplings cooked this way. But then the goose was always dismembered before it was put into the pot with the dumplings.

The Michaelmas goose is usually what is known as a 'green goose', that is it has been feeding on the stubble after the harvest is gathered, which makes it very good to eat. The way to choose a goose is given in Dean Swift's poem 'The Progress of Poetry':

The farmer's goose, who in the stubble,
Has fed without restraint or trouble,
Grown fat with corn and sitting still,
Can scarce get o'er the barndoor still;
And hardly waddles forth to cool
Her belly in the neighb'ring pool:
Nor loudly cackles at the door;
For cackling shows the goose is poor.

The Irish Folklore Commission has an interesting account of how the Christmas goose was cooked over the turf fire around the turn of the twentieth century and possibly earlier in County Clare.

The Christmas goose was cooked thus; put the goose into a pot half-filled with cold water; hang over the fire till the water boils; take off and place on iron bar and/or stand beside the fire with coals under for about one hour. Then place coals on top; baste from time to time; add parsnips to the side of the goose and put slices of bacon on top of the goose. The fire must be kept good for this cooking. The top (breast) side will be a beautiful golden brown when well done.

Wipe over the goose joints and prick the breast skin with a thin fork, then roll in seasoned flour. Heat the goose fat and turn the joints in it until they are brown all over. Transfer to a large heavy pot and brown the vegetables in the same fat. Arrange these round the goose and sprinkle with sage. Heat the stock and pour into the pot, bring to the boil, cover and simmer for about 1 ½ hours.

Meanwhile, make the dumplings. Mix all the dumpling ingredients together, then add enough water to make a soft yet pliable dough. With floured hands roll into small balls. Put the balls in the pot with the goose and cook for a further half hour, adding a very little more liquid to the pan if necessary.

Serve the goose on a large warmed dish with the vegetables and dumplings arranged around the edges. The goose can be left whole and stuffed with cooked potatoes mixed with onion, chopped bacon, the goose liver and herbs.

SERVES 10–12

1 goose, about 4 ½ kg (10 lb), jointed

seasoned flour

2 tablespoons goose fat

2 large onions, stuck with cloves

5–6 medium-sized carrots, sliced

2–3 medium-sized parsnips, chopped

1 head celery, chopped

pinch dried sage

1 litre (1 ¾ pints) giblet stock

DUMPLINGS

225 g (8 oz) flour

110 g (4 oz) shredded suet

1 teaspoon salt

pinch ground nutmeg

1 tablespoon parsley, chopped

Braised Rabbit

1 rabbit, jointed and marinated

3 tablespoons oil

1 large onion, sliced

3–4 carrots, sliced

flour

pinch powdered marjoram

salt and pepper

600 ml (1 pint) chicken stock or half stock, half cider

Rabbit was a great food for country people for many years. Tomás O'Crohan in *The Islandman* tells us of the many rabbits they caught on the Blasket Islands when he was young: 'When we had all come to the boat and put the game together, we had eight dozen rabbits – a dozen a-piece.' Maurice O'Sullivan in *Twenty Years A-Growing* writes of the same island and rabbit stew: 'We sat down to dinner, a savoury dinner it was – a fine stew of rabbits and plenty of soup.' Young rabbits can be roasted – as with the body of the hare – and wrapped in bacon.

Pat the joints dry. Heat the oil and fry the joints on all sides until brown. Lift out and put into a casserole. In the same oil lightly fry the vegetables, add the marjoram, sprinkle a little flour over and stir. Add the stock gradually, stirring until smooth, then stir in a few tablespoons of the marinade. Pour this over the rabbit, cover and cook in a moderate oven at 180°C/350°F/ gas mark 4 for about half an hour, then lower the heat to 150°C/300°F/gas mark 2 for a further 1 ½ hours or until tender.

SERVES ABOUT 6

Rabbit Pie

The Braised Rabbit recipe above can be used as the basis for a delicious rabbit pie.

Take the meat when cooked from the bones, add 2 or 3 rashers of chopped bacon, fill the stock to come up to within 2.5 cm (1 in) of the rim of the dish, then cover with rich shortcrust or flaky pastry (see page 260) and cook for about half an hour.

SERVES ABOUT 6

CHEAPER CUTS

By THEODORA FITZGIBBON

THE BEST BEEF for any kind of stew is the shin: not only is it the cheapest, but it has more flavour, very little fat, no bone, and tendons which when fully cooked give both taste and a gelatinous quality to the dish. It is excellent for any sort of braise and makes an excellent goulash.

GOULASH to serve four

3 lb. shin of beef chopped into cubes
1 chuck of marrow bone if possible, not essential
2 tablespoons oil
2 large onions
1 heaped tablespoon flour
2 large sliced carrots
1 clove garlic
1 bayleaf
1 tablespoon tomato purée
2 tablespoons paprika
1 teaspoon powdered marjoram
2 teaspoons caraway seeds
water
1 glass red wine
salt and pepper
yoghurt

Heat the oil and fry the meat and onions in it until they are soft and brown, then add the marrow bone and brown on both sides. Shake the flour over, add the wine and about one pint water, stir well and add other ingredients. Cover, and cook in a slow to moderate oven (250°F.) for about two and a half hours, checking that it does not run dry of liquid. Just before serving dig the marrow from the bone if you have used it, stir it in, and add about four tablespoons plain yoghurt. Serve with boiled potatoes or boiled, buttered noodles. Sometimes in Hungary the potatoes are added to the stew about a half hour before it is ready.

●

OXTAIL, although strictly speaking not a cut of beef is nevertheless a very cheap and good meal if cooked well. It must be trimmed of as much fat as possible for otherwise it can be greasy. I always cook it the day before it is needed so that the fat can be skimmed from the top when it is cold. If you have a large family and feel that one oxtail won't be enough, it makes a good rich stew if two or three lamb's kidneys are added.

1 chopped oxtail
3 lamb's kidneys (optional)
2 large onions
1 bayleaf
2 tablespoons oil
1 teaspoon marjoram
1 heaped tablespoon flour
1 glass red wine
1 pint beef stock (a cube will do)
1 lb. sliced carrots

tomatoes (about ½ lb.) can be added to the braise about a half hour before it is ready.

PRESSED BEEF FLANK

3 lb. beef flank
1 teaspoon black peppercorns
¼ lb. bacon rashers or 1 lb. pork
Sausagemeat
2 bayleaves
¼ pint stock and ½ pint water
salt and pepper

Pressure cooking time is 35 minutes.

Remove any superfluous fat from the meat and lay it out flat, line it with the bacon or sausagemeat, bayleaves and seasonings, then roll it up and tie securely. Put into a large saucepan or casserole, cover with the stock and water, and simmer slowly for about four hours or until the meat is so soft it will shred with a fork. Take out the meat and put into a dish which just fits it, add a little of the stock, cover with foil and weight the top, then put into a cold place overnight. Serve cold, cut into thin slices with a sauce made from 3 parts oil to one of wine vinegar, with chopped capers and chopped fresh herbs in it.

●

PICKLED PORK is an old-fashioned meal these days, but one which can be extremely good. Use either streaky, or belly of pork, which can be roasted until crisp and is delicious, or simmered in one piece as a stew. It is particularly good cooked with rabbit, which I am glad to see again at a fairly reasonable price. Use plenty of onions, a bayleaf and parsley; cider is good mixed with half water as a stock. Season well, and cook gently for about 2 hours. If liked the rabbit can be taken from the bone when cool and layered with the pork in a deep dish. If the liquid is poured around it will jelly when cold and make a superb terrine.

HAND OF PICKLED PORK is another favourite of mine, but there is not a lot of meat on one. You will need two if your family is over 3 people.

2 hands pork
1 large onion
pinch of sugar
1 lb. split peas
sprig of thyme
pepper

Soak the pork overnight, and also the split peas. Put the pork into a large saucepan with the sugar, sliced onion and the thyme, water to barely cover, and let it come gently to the boil. Remove any scum on top with a spoon, then let the pork simmer gently for about 35 minutes. Strain the split peas (the green ones are best) then add them to the pork liquor, and cook them at a good simmering pace

PRESSUR

CASSOULET (Serves 4-6).
1 lb. dried haricot beans soaked overnight in cold water
to cover meat, poultry or s etc. (see below)
3 cloves garlic
2 medium onions
2 tablespoons tomato puree
2 level tablespoons brown sugar
a good pinch of marjoram a paprika
1 glass red wine (optional) and
¼ lb. ham or bacon chopped
salt and pepper

Put all ingredients in the pressur and add water to about 1 inch top of the drained beans. Put th bring up to pressure and cook minutes. Leave the cooker to co ally and then remove the valve. beans into a large casserole, taste soning and then add whatever r

a mixture) you have available : pi lamb, park, chicken, goose (par good), duck, or more chopped ham, and sausages, either frankfurters ordinary kind. (If the latter grill t a minute just to brown the outsic the lid on and put into a modera (approx. 325°F.) for about ½ hour be left considerably longer if p lower temperature. If it is too liq add a handful of coarse fresh brea and leave the lid off. Push the brea down at least twice to sop up th Likewise if it is too dry then add more wine or water or a mixture

Cassoulet can be made well in and is all the better for re-heat two or three times. In my house gets a chance for it goes like a f

GREEN SPLIT PEA SOUP (serv
1 lb. green split peas
(yellow can also be used bu seem to me to have quite as good a taste)
1 tablespoon flour
2 chopped rashers bacon, or a ham bone
1 large onion
1 tablespoon oil
1 tablespoon Worcestershire sa
1½ quarts of water, but prefera ham or corned beef stock skimmed of fat
salt and pepper

It is not necessary to soak overnight, but if they are whole be soaked and drained before c

Heat the oil and lightly fry onion, add the chopped bacon crisp slightly Add all ingredie

Venison en Daube

This is a French recipe using the cheapest part of the deer – the shoulder.

Keep the bones and put them in a saucepan with the sliced carrots and onion, bay leaf and thyme. Cover with cold water and simmer for about 1 hour. Then cool and strain, but reserve the stock and reduce it to 1.1 litre (2 pints).

Meanwhile, trim and cut the meat and bacon into cubes, dredge with flour, then heat the oil or butter. Fry the bacon until the fat runs out and it browns slightly, push aside and add the venison cubes and brown them, too.

Prepare the remaining onion and carrots, and layer in the casserole, then follow with the bacon and meat on top, and sprinkle with more flour. Then season the stock to taste and heat up. Pour over, cover closely and cook at 180°C/350°F/ gas mark 4 for about 2 hours. Test for tenderness and taste. If ready, add the wine and redcurrant jelly, cover and cook again for about half an hour.

SERVES 4

1 shoulder boned venison, reserve bones
2 onions (1 sliced for stock)
1 bay leaf
225 g (8 oz) bacon trimmings
5 carrots (2–3 sliced for stock)
salt and black pepper
3 tablespoons oil or margarine
a little flour
sprig thyme
2 tablespoons redcurrant jelly
1 glass red wine or port wine

MEAT

'When I remarked to the butcher that all the animals seemed to be born without tongues, tails, hearts, kidneys, liver or balls, he winked at me, a great arm went under the counter, and flung up a half-frozen oxtail.'

Beef Stew with Dumplings

900 g (2 lb) stewing beef, shin or chuck, cut into cubes

seasoned flour

2 tablespoons beef dripping or oil

3–4 medium-sized onions, chopped

6 small carrots, sliced

1 bay leaf

1 sprig thyme

1 sprig parsley

salt and pepper

850 ml (1 ½ pints) stock

DUMPLINGS

4 tablespoons flour

2 tablespoons fresh breadcrumbs

2 tablespoons grated suet

1 tablespoon mixed herbs, chopped

In Tipperary, which formerly was not a sheep-raising county, this was often called 'Irish stew', but genuine Irish stew is made with lamb or mutton. A little chopped bacon may be added to this, as well as a small, chopped swede if liked.

Roll the meat in the seasoned flour. Heat the fat or oil and quickly brown the meat. Put with the vegetables, herbs and seasoning into a saucepan. Add the stock, bring to the boil and simmer gently for 1–1 ½ hours or until tender.

Meanwhile, make the dumplings. Combine the dumpling ingredients, roll into small balls and chill. When the meat is tender, add the dumplings, bring back to the boil and simmer uncovered for about 10 minutes, then serve.

SERVES 4

Beefsteak and Kidney Pie

Heat the dripping or oil and quickly fry the beef and kidney, turning to brown all over. Take out and put into a saucepan. Soften the sliced onion in the same fat and crumble the stock cube into the pan with a sprinkling of flour. Add the marjoram, mixed spice and seasoning, then mix well. Add about 600 ml (1 pint) of water and stir until thick.

Pour the mixture over the meat, bring to the boil, cover and simmer until the meat is tender, about 1 ½ hours. Transfer to a 1-litre (2-pint) pie dish, allowing the liquid to come no higher than 1 cm (½ in) from the top. Dampen the rim of the pie dish, roll the pastry out to the right size, lay over and press down the edges with a fork or a pastry crimper. Make a small hole in the top and cover it lightly with a small rosette made from the pastry scraps. Brush with milk and bake at 200°C/400°F/gas mark 6 for 15 minutes, then lower heat to 180°C/350°F/gas mark 4 for a further 15 minutes.

SERVES 4

VARIATION: If liked, mushrooms can be added just before putting on the pastry crust.

700 g (1 ½ lb) stewing beef, cut in cubes

350 g (12 oz) ox kidney, skinned, fatty core removed, chopped

2 tablespoons beef dripping or oil

1 large onion, sliced

1 beef stock cube

flour

pinch ground marjoram

pinch mixed spice

salt and pepper

225 g (8 oz) shortcrust pastry (see page 260)

milk for brushing

Braised Beef with Prunes

1.1 kg (2 ½ lb) stewing beef

1 large onion, sliced

1 tablespoon oil

1 large garlic clove, chopped

salt and pepper

1 rounded tablespoon flour

300 ml (½ pint) dark beer or Guinness

a little water

225 g (8 oz) prunes, soaked and stoned (ready-to-eat prunes can also be used)

grilled hazelnuts, optional

Trim the beef and cut into convenient serving pieces – do not dice. Heat the oil and fry the meat quickly on both sides, then add the sliced onion, shake over the flour and mix well, cooking for 1 minute. Pour over the beer and chopped garlic, and season to taste. Add enough water to make the sauce to a thickness you like. Cover and braise 170°C/325°F/gas mark 3 for about 1 ½ hours.

If using the hazelnuts, grill lightly, then stuff one into each prune. Take out the casserole and put the prunes into it. Cover, put back in the oven and continue cooking for about 30 minutes.

SERVES ABOUT 4–5

Roast Beef with Batter Pudding

1.8 kg (4 lb) sirloin or best rib beef, bone in

2 tablespoons beef dripping or oil

mixed herbs

black pepper

240 ml (8 fl oz) cider, beef stock or red wine

boiling beef dripping

BATTER

4 rounded tablespoons flour

½ teaspoon salt

1 large egg, beaten

300 ml (½ pint) milk

Batter pudding is the Irish version of Yorkshire pudding. Many Irish like their meat quite well cooked, which rather spoils a good joint of beef in my opinion. A largish piece of beef cooked in this way will have the best flavour, as small joints are disappointing.

Preheat the oven to 200°C/400°F/gas mark 6. Heat the fat and quickly sear the beef on all sides to seal in the juices. Put into a roasting pan with the dripping or oil, and sprinkle the herbs and black pepper over the meat. Put into the hot oven and cook for half an hour. As soon as the meat is in the oven, make the batter.

Sift the flour and salt, and make a well in the middle. Add the beaten egg and half the milk, and beat for about 5 minutes to form a smooth paste. Add the remaining milk and beat for a further 5 minutes (3 minutes will do with an electric beater). Leave uncovered in a cool place until required. After the meat has cooked for half an hour, lower the heat to 190°C/375°F/gas mark 5. Baste, then continue to cook for a total roasting time of 16 minutes to the pound (450 g) for rare beef, 20 minutes for medium, or longer for well done.

Half an hour before the end of the beef roasting time, cook the batter. Pour about 2 tablespoons of the hot beef dripping from the roasting pan into a fairly shallow tin about 18 cm (7 in) square. Add a few drops of cold water to the cold batter and beat it for a moment, then pour the batter into the fat – it should sizzle as it goes in. Put the tin at the very top of the hot oven for about 30 minutes.

When the beef is done, remove from the oven, put onto a warmed serving dish and keep warm. Scrape down the sides of the roasting pan and add the cider, beef stock or red wine over heat. Stir well, season and boil up quickly to reduce.

Serve very hot with the roast beef and batter pudding, which should be served as soon as it has risen or, like a soufflé, it will fall.

SERVES ABOUT 8

Collard Beef

The name is a contraction of 'collared beef', possibly because it was often served cold surrounded by salad vegetables such as watercress, cucumber and pickles. It was a popular dish in Ireland when I was a child and always served at Christmas.

Trim the beef of fat, bone and gristle, and cut it across horizontally into three pieces, laying each one out flat. Sprinkle the first piece with salt and pepper and half the spices, then lay 2 bacon rashers on top. Place the second piece of beef over the bacon and repeat, placing the third slice on top. Press down well and wrap tightly, either in double foil or muslin, and secure well by twisting the foil or tying with twine if using muslin. Put into a large saucepan and cover with water. Bring gently to the boil, then simmer for 3–4 hours. Cool slightly, then take out and remove the foil or muslin. Put into a dish that it just fits, put a plate over it and a weight on top. Chill then serve.

SERVES ABOUT 8

1 ½–2 kg (3 ¼–4 ½ lb) beef, silverside or topside

salt and pepper

4 rashers streaky bacon

½ teaspoon each allspice, whole peppercorns, sage and thyme

sprinkling ground clove, nutmeg and ginger

2 bay leaves

Steak au Poivre

This is a very aromatic dish, which is not hot despite the peppercorns.

Grind or crush the peppercorns and press on both sides of the steaks, so that they are well covered. (If the steaks are very large, you may need more, but you will be the best judge.) Melt the butter in a heavy pan and fry the steaks carefully on both sides so that the peppercorns do not become dislodged. The pan must be hot enough to make the steaks sizzle as they are put in, and if a very rare steak is preferred, the butter can be quite browned. When done to your liking, warm the brandy in a ladle over a candle or a lighter, pour over the steaks and then ignite. When the flames have died down, serve at once.

SERVES 4

4 steaks, either fillet or sirloin

2 tablespoons black or green peppercorns, coarsely crushed

1 tablespoon butter

2 tablespoons brandy, warmed

Wellington Steak

450 g (1 lb) flaky pastry
(see page 260)

1 fillet steak, about 1 ¼ kg
(2 ¾ lb)

450 g (1 lb) mushrooms,
finely chopped

salt and pepper

175 g (6 oz) butter

1 egg, beaten to glaze

This was said to be a favourite of the Duke of Wellington,
who was born in Ireland, and it is sometimes also known as
beef Wellington. It is good for a whole beef fillet and makes
an excellent party dish.

Make the pastry first and chill until needed. Trim the fat from
the fillet, then season, rub with butter and put at the top of a
very hot oven at 220°C/425°F/gas mark 7 for 10 minutes.
Heat the rest of the butter and sweat the mushrooms until
they form a purée. Drain off any excess fat, then roll the steak
in the mushrooms so that all surfaces are covered.

Roll out the pastry into a shape large enough to fit the steak
and to meet at the top. Lay the meat on it, bring up over
the top to enclose the meat, dampen the pastry edges and
squeeze together to secure. Brush with the beaten egg,
then place on a baking sheet and put in a very hot oven
220°C/425°F/gas mark 7 for 15–20 minutes or until
golden.

SERVES 4–5

Crusty Roast Lamb

Wipe the lamb over and cut criss-cross slits around the top. Mix together the breadcrumbs, herbs, butter, salt and pepper. Rub the mixture on to the top of the meat, pressing down well so that it sticks. Fill the bottom of the roasting pan with the vegetables and apple, mixing and seasoning well. Put the joint on top, then pour the stock into the pan but not over the meat.

Cover loosely with a piece of foil and bake at 200°C/400°F/gas mark 6 for half an hour. Then lower the heat to 180°C/350°F/gas mark 4 and cook for a further 20–25 minutes to the pound (450 g). Take off the foil before the final half hour and check that the vegetables are nearly cooked. Finish the cooking without the foil, to let the top get brown and crusty.

SERVES ABOUT 6

1 shoulder lamb, about 1 ½–2 kg (3 ¼–4 ½ lb)

1 cup fresh breadcrumbs

pinch mixed herbs

2 tablespoons butter, soft

salt and pepper

700 g (1 ½ lb) potatoes, peeled and sliced

1 large onion, sliced

1 large cooking apple, peeled, cored and sliced

300 ml (½ pint) chicken stock

Osso Buco

Heat the butter, margarine or oil in a large pan and lightly fry the onion, then add the pieces of shin of veal (with the bone and the marrow inside) and brown them quickly on both sides – ensure that they are standing up, otherwise the marrow will spill out. Pour the white wine around and let it bubble up for about 5 minutes. Transfer this to a casserole, add one of the garlic cloves, tomatoes, stock, salt and pepper, then cover and cook in a slow oven for 2 hours, taking off the lid for the last half hour. Meanwhile, grate the peel of the lemon very finely, add the chopped parsley and the other very finely chopped clove of garlic. Put this mixture – known as gremolata in Italy – on top 10 minutes before serving.

SERVES 6

1.8 kg (4 lb) shin veal, sawn into pieces about 5 cm (2 in) (but check that it has a good coating of meat around it)

150 ml (¼ pint) white wine

300 ml (½ pint) stock (a stock cube will do)

450 g (1 lb) tomatoes, skinned and chopped, or equivalent tin

2 cloves garlic

1 large lemon

4 tablespoons chopped parsley

75 g (3 oz) butter or margarine or 3 tablespoons olive oil

1 medium-sized onion, peeled and sliced

salt and pepper

Irish Stew

1 ¼–1 ½ kg (2 ¾–3 ¼ lb)
best end of neck chops

900 g (2 lb) potatoes,
peeled and sliced

450 g (1 lb) onions, sliced

1 tablespoon parsley, chopped

pinch thyme

salt and pepper

about 600 ml (1 pint) stock

This dish is known all over the Western world and is very likely one of the oldest Irish recipes in existence, but it is frequently spoilt by too much liquid. Other vegetables and barley are sometimes added but in my opinion do not improve it.

Trim the meat of bone, fat and gristle, then cut into fairly large pieces. Layer the meat and vegetables in a deep pan, add the herbs and season each layer well, then end with the potatoes. Pour in the stock and cover with a piece of buttered foil, then the lid, and bake in a slow oven at 150°C/300°F/gas mark 2 for about 2 hours. Or, if preferred, cook on the top of the stove or cooker, shaking the pan from time to time to prevent sticking. Add a very little more liquid if needed.

SERVES 4

Rogan Josh

Rogan Josh is a mild northern Indian curry which can be used for any meats, chicken, fish, prawns or eggs. It has a creamy, delicious flavour.

Heat the oil or butter and lightly brown the onion, then add the garlic, turmeric, garam masala and all the other spices. Fry for a few minutes, then add the lamb and brown all over. Stir in the yoghurt, season with salt and add the tomatoes and water. Cover and simmer very gently until the meat is tender and the sauce thick. Garnish with the herbs and cardamom before serving.

SERVES 4–6 WITH SIDE DISHES

900 g (2 lb) leg of lamb, cubed

1 teaspoon ground ginger

1 tablespoon garam masala

1 tablespoon ground coriander (*dhaniya*)

pinch saffron, optional

150 ml (¼ pint) plain yoghurt

3 tablespoons oil or butter

salt

1 large onion, thinly sliced

3 cloves garlic

pinch each cayenne pepper, mace, nutmeg and paprika

3 large peeled and chopped tomatoes or canned

150 ml (¼ pint) water

1 teaspoon turmeric

fresh marjoram or parsley to garnish, chopped

pinch freshly ground cardamom

Lamb Shoulder in Pastry

350 g (12 oz) shortcrust or flaky pastry (see page 260)

1 tablespoon mixed chopped herbs such as parsley, chives and rosemary or marjoram

1 ¼–1 ½ kg (2 ¾–3 ¼ lb) boned shoulder of lamb

6 tablespoons butter

salt and black pepper

milk or beaten egg to glaze

Make the pastry and chill for at least 1 hour before using. See that the lamb is fairly free of fat, then securely tie, put in a baking tin and rub with about a third of the butter. Put into a very hot oven at 230°C/450°F/gas mark 8 for 20–30 minutes. Take out and let cool a little in the baking tin.

Mix the remaining butter with the herbs, salt and pepper. Roll out the pastry to a piece large enough to wrap round the joint. Carefully remove the string from the lamb, trying to retain the shape. Put the lamb in the centre of the pastry, dampen the edges and draw the pastry up over the top and secure well by squeezing the pastry ends and edges together. Turn over so that the fold is underneath and put on a baking sheet. Decorate with pastry leaves made from the trimmings if liked. Prick all over the top lightly with a fork, then brush with either the milk or the beaten egg.

Put into a hot oven at 200°C/400°F/gas mark 6 and cook for about half an hour uncovered, then cover with foil and cook for a further 25 minutes or until the pastry is nicely browned. Turn the sheet around once during cooking so that both sides bake evenly. Cut into fairly thick slices and serve.

SERVES ABOUT 6

Honeyed Lamb

1.4–1.8 kg (3–4 lb) shoulder of lamb, scored diamond fashion with a sharp knife

level tablespoon fresh rosemary, chopped, or 1 teaspoon dried

salt and freshly ground black pepper

1 teaspoon ground ginger

225 g (8 oz) thick honey

approx. 300 ml (½ pint) hot cider

Welsh lamb is small and renowned for its sweetness.

First line the baking tin with foil to prevent the honey from sticking. Rub the shoulder all over with salt, pepper and the ginger, put into the baking tin and sprinkle with half the chopped rosemary. Coat the top skin with honey and pour the hot cider around. Bake in a hot oven at 200°C/400°F/gas mark 6 for half an hour, then lower to 180°C/350°F/gas mark 4 for a further 1 ¼ hours, checking halfway through that it is not drying up – if so, add some more warmed cider. Baste at least once, then 15 minutes before serving, add the remaining rosemary to the top. To serve, put the lamb onto a warmed serving dish and keep warm. Boil up the pan juices to reduce slightly and serve the gravy separately.

SERVES 6–8

VARIATION: Chicken or pork can be cooked the same way, but the chicken should first be lightly browned in a little oil.

Stuffed Lambs' Hearts

This good country dish remains popular.

Wash the hearts and remove any fat, pipes or bits of gristle.
Make a cut from the top down on one side so that it forms
a pocket. Combine the soaked breadcrumbs with the lemon
rind, onion, thyme, parsley, marjoram, salt and pepper. Mix
well, then stuff the hearts and secure. Melt the fat and quickly
brown the hearts all over, shaking over about a tablespoon
of flour. Let the flour brown a minute, then add the onion
and celery, turning in the fat over a moderate heat. Gradually
add the stock to barely cover the hearts, adding a little more
water if necessary. Put in the bay leaf and mace, transfer
everything to a casserole, then cover and cook in a slow oven
at 160°C/325°F/gas mark 3 for 1 ½–2 hours.

SERVES 4

4 lambs' hearts

110 g (4 oz) breadcrumbs,
soaked in a little milk

grated rind of 1 lemon

1 small onion, grated or
finely chopped

1 teaspoon each fresh thyme,
parsley and marjoram, chopped,
or ½ teaspoon dried

salt and pepper

2 tablespoons fat or oil

about 1 tablespoon flour

1 large onion, coarsely chopped

1 stick celery, chopped

1 bay leaf

pinch mace

600 ml (1 pint) stock

Gigot au Pastis

This is leg of mutton with Pernod or any other anise-based spirit, where one double measure at least is required for this dish.

Make several slits in the leg of mutton and insert the slices of garlic. Smear with olive oil and sprinkle over the chopped rosemary and small thyme leaves. Roast in a moderate oven at 180°C/350°F/gas mark 4 for 15 minutes to the pound (450 g) for rare meat and 20–25 minutes for well done. Add salt and pepper after cooking. On the table, or just before serving, gently warm the Pernod or pastis in a ladle, set it alight and pour over the mutton so that it is enveloped in fragrant flames.

SERVES 8–10

2.2 kg (5 lb) leg of mutton
2 cloves garlic, peeled and sliced
few sprigs rosemary, chopped
2 sprigs thyme
3 tablespoons olive oil
1 double Pernod to set alight

Mutton Pies

PASTRY

900 g (2 lb) self-raising flour

225 g (8 oz) butter

110 g (4 oz) lard or
mutton dripping

1 heaped teaspoon salt

FILLING

pinch thyme

900 g (2 lb) lean mutton

salt and pepper

1 small onion, grated or
finely chopped

2 teaspoons fresh mint,
chopped, or 1 teaspoon dried

milk to glaze

These pies, also called 'Dingle pies' and somewhat like the Cornish pasty, are traditional in Co. Kerry. They could be bought in Dingle every August at the Puck Fair in Killorglin. The 'king' of the fair is a large puck goat, much decorated and garlanded by greenery, which is hoisted high above the crowds onto a covered platform where he remains chained by the horns throughout the fair, munching on cabbages.

Legend has it that it commemorates a time when the noise of a herd of goats led by the puck, or billy, ran into town and warned the Irish of the advancing English soldiers, but it is much more probable that the origins are far earlier than that and come from the puck being a symbol of fertility and good luck. The 12 August is Old Lammas and Lammas Day, 1 August, was formerly known in Ireland as 'Lewy's Fair' in memory of a pre-Christian deity, Lugh, the god of light. The main business of the Puck Fair is the sale of livestock and it is also a traditional gathering place for the travelling community.

To make the pastry, mix the salt into the sifted flour, then rub in the fats and gradually add about a cup of water, mixing well, until the dough is firm but not dry. Roll into a ball and chill.

Trim the meat of fat and gristle, and if you can tell that it is tender, use it raw, but if you are in any doubt, boil it in water to cover for half an hour, together with any bones you have trimmed off. Cut it into very small pieces, season well and mix with the onion and herbs.

Roll out more than half the pastry on a lightly floured surface and cut into 12 circles about 10 cm (4 in) across. Roll out the remaining pastry and cut into 12 slightly smaller circles. Put about a twelfth of the meat mixture onto each of the smaller circles, dampen the outer edges, then lay a larger circle on top of each. Press down and crimp with the prongs of a dampened fork. Make a small slit in the top of each to let the steam out and brush with a little milk. Put onto a greased baking sheet and bake at 180°C/350°F/gas mark 4 for 15 minutes. Lower the heat to 160°C/325°F/gas mark 3 and cook for a further 45 minutes if you used raw meat; reduce the cooking time by 20 minutes if it was cooked.

MAKES 12

Roast Lamb Shanks

4 lamb shanks

2 medium-sized onions or shallots, chopped

50 g (2 oz) grated hard cheese

salt and pepper

110 g (4 oz) mushrooms

parsley

oil or butter

Take 4 pieces of foil large enough to wrap up each shank securely, then put 1 shank on each piece, and add a little onion, mushrooms, seasoning and parsley. Either rub the foil with butter or pour a little oil over, sprinkle each one with cheese and wrap up well. Put into a baking tin and cook in a moderate to hot oven (190°C/375°F/gas mark 5) and roast for about 1 hour. Serve each shank in its foil with a jacket-baked potato, sprinkled with fresh herbs and served with ice-cold plain yoghurt.

ALLOW 1 PER PERSON

Pork Císte

This traditional Irish dish is a kind of pork pudding not very often seen today but is extremely good. The name is confusing, as císte can also mean cake in Irish, and some loaves of bread are also called cake, both in Irish and English. It is also made with lamb or mutton.

Put the chops around the inside edge of a medium-sized flameproof pan with any bone-ends sticking upwards. Skin and chop the kidneys or liver and add to the centre, along with the vegetables and herbs. Season well and add just enough stock to barely cover the vegetables. Cover, bring to the boil, lower heat and simmer gently for about 30 minutes.

Meanwhile, make the císte by mixing together the flour, salt, suet and baking powder and adding enough milk to make a firm dough. Add the sultanas and mix well. On a lightly floured surface, roll out to the size of the pan, place it on top, then press down to meet the stew – even if the bones stick through – leaving about 2.5 cm (1 in) of space above to allow for rising. Cover with greased wax paper and the lid, and cook over low heat for 1–1 ½ hours.

When ready, loosen the edges with a knife and cut into wedges in order to serve the meat, vegetables and císte in each portion.

SERVES 4–6

4 pork chops, trimmed of fat
3 pork kidneys or 225 g (8 oz) pork liver
2 medium-sized onions, sliced
2 medium-sized carrots, sliced
1 tablespoon parsley, chopped
pinch thyme
salt and pepper
about 600 ml (1 pint) stock
225 g (8 oz) flour
salt
1 teaspoon baking powder
110 g (4 oz) grated suet
about 120 ml (4 fl oz) milk
2–3 tablespoons sultanas

Roast Pork and Apple Sauce

1.8 kg (4 lb) joint pork

600 ml (1 pint) cider, stock
or water

salt and pepper

SAUCE

450 g (1 lb) cooking apples

about 1 tablespoon sugar

pinch ground nutmeg or cloves

1 rounded tablespoon butter,
cut into small pieces

Several different joints of pork are suitable for roasting, such as leg, shoulder or loin – it is really a matter of taste and pocket. The shoulder is usually boned and rolled and is a very sweet part of the pig. The stuffing recipe below can be used if wanted, but make sure to ask the butcher to make a cavity or pocket in the pork for you.

The special delight of some joints of pork is the crispy skin known as 'crackling'. This should be well scored by the butcher and an important part of the cooking is to see that the skin should never come into contact with the hot fat during cooking or it will fry and become what the Norman archers called *cuir bouilli*, boiled leather. They used it to make breastplates to withstand the battleaxes and arrows of the enemy!

Put the pork into a roasting pan and place in a very hot oven at 220°C/425°F/gas mark 7, without any added fat, and cook for 30 minutes, then take out and pour off the fat into a bowl. Lower the heat to 200°C/400°F/gas mark 6, put back into the oven with the cider, chicken stock or water, and cook for 30 minutes to the pound (450 g). About 30 minutes before it is ready, remove from the oven and sprinkle salt over the skin and shake a few drops of cold water over the top, then continue cooking in the oven. This will give a very good crispy crackling. The liquid should be reduced on top of the stove and seasoned to taste.

Peel, core and slice the apples, then cook in about 4 tablespoons of water until they are quite soft. Either sieve or mash well, and heat up again. Add sugar to taste, the nutmeg or cloves and the butter. Serve hot. This apple sauce is good with pork, duck, goose, mackerel and some game.

SERVES ABOUT 6–8

Mix all the stuffing ingredients together and moisten with a little milk: see that it is well absorbed and in no way sloppy. Pack the stuffing into the cavity or pocket the butcher has made for you, roll the pork over and secure well. Rub all over with butter and season lightly. Then put into a roasting tin and follow the instructions above for cooking.

STUFFING

2 cups fresh white breadcrumbs

1 medium-sized onion, finely chopped

1 teaspoon grated lemon rind

juice of ½ lemon

pinch ground mace or nutmeg

½ teaspoon sage

½ teaspoon thyme

1 tablespoon parsley, chopped

about 2 tablespoons milk

salt and pepper

Stuffed Pork Chops

It is from the Irish that the word 'griskin' comes, meaning the best part of the loin. Some idea of the usefulness of the pig is given in this extract from *The Irish Journals of Elizabeth Smith, 1840–50*, of Baltiboys House, Blessington.

> *NOVEMBER 20TH, 1842*
> *A present from old Peggy, the back griskins of her pig ... it will be the most delicious bacon ever cured, but all the comfort that so small a weight of consumable material will give, the skin for a sieve, the lard for kitchen and the bones for soup, the blood for puddings, and the inmeats, a week's dinners, it will be a very merry Christmas ...*

4 lean pork chops
black pepper
4 large onions, peeled and sliced
50 g (2 oz) butter
1 teaspoon sugar
1 tablespoon flour, seasoned
150 ml (¼ pint) warm milk
2 tablespoons cream
4 tablespoons breadcrumbs
1 tablespoon butter

Trim the chops and take out the small piece of bone, then put onto a grilling pan and dust with black pepper. Peel and slice the onions into a saucepan, just cover with water and bring to the boil, then simmer for 10 minutes. Drain, but reserve the liquid. Heat the butter in another pan, then add the onions and sugar, and cook until they are quite soft. Beat with a fork to purée them. Add the flour and let it cook for a minute, then add the warm milk and enough of the onion liquor to make a thickish sauce. Season well, then add the cream.

Grill the chops well on one side only, transfer cooked side down into a roasting pan and cover the tops with the onion sauce. Sprinkle breadcrumbs on top, then a dot of butter and pepper. Put into a hot oven at 220°C/425°F/gas mark 7 for about 20 minutes or until the top is crisply browned. If liked, the chops can be grilled in the usual way and the sauce served with them, but the crispy topping above is very good.

SERVES 4

Ham Cooked with Guinness and Served with Apple Sauce

1.4–1.8 kg (3–4 lb) shoulder bacon

½ lemon

pepper

about 450 g (1 lb) mixed root vegetables

1 tablespoon black treacle or brown sugar

300 ml (½ pint) Guinness

SAUCE

450 g (1 lb) cooking apples

about 2–3 celery stalks, chopped, optional

pinch ginger

about 2 whole cloves

1 cup of water

sugar to taste

Soak the bacon in cold water overnight, then drain and scrape the skin well. Make a bed of root vegetables in the bottom of a saucepan or casserole, and lay the bacon on top. Add the lemon, treacle or brown sugar, and pepper, then barely cover with cold water. Gradually bring to the boil, then turn down to the merest glimmer and cook for about 25 minutes to the ½ kg (1 lb), but test towards the end of the cooking time. At the last half an hour add the Guinness, bring back to the boil and continue cooking.

Meanwhile, make the apple sauce and keep hot. Peel, core and slice the cooking apples. Add the chopped celery stalks, ginger and whole cloves. Add not more than the 1 cup of water, then simmer until soft. Add sugar to taste, but do not make it too sweet, for it should contrast with the sweet bacon or ham.

SERVES ABOUT 8

Stuffed Shoulder or Collar of Bacon with Apricot and Orange Sauce

First soak the bacon in cold water overnight. The next day throw away the water and barely cover with more cold water. Add the lemon and parsley to the water and boil, then simmer for about 1 ½ hours. Take out of the water and remove the skin and any excess fat.

Meanwhile, to make the stuffing, lightly sauté the mushrooms and mash the apricots in their own juice, then mix with the almonds or walnuts, breadcrumbs and egg.

When the bacon is ready, put it in an ovenproof dish and roll the stuffing into small balls, putting these into the apricot halves. Place these around the joint. Mix the orange juice, apricot juice and honey, then pour over. Cover loosely with foil and bake at 180°C/350°F/gas mark 4 for about 40 minutes.

Pour off the liquid when the joint is ready and add the 150 ml (¼ pint) of orange juice and about 2 tablespoons of mashed canned apricots. Mix this very well, then cream the cornflour with a little water and add to the pan gradually, stirring after each addition until it is the desired thickness. Do not make it too thick, just slightly so. Pour some over the joint and the stuffed apricots and serve the rest separately.

SERVES 6–8

1.4–1.6 kg (3–3 ½ lb) bacon

½ lemon

sprig parsley

350 g (12 oz) drained canned apricots (reserving the juice)

3 tablespoons orange juice

3 tablespoons reserved apricot juice (above)

1 rounded tablespoon honey

STUFFING

50 g (2 oz) mushrooms, chopped

50 g (2 oz) canned apricots in their own juice, mashed

50 g (2 oz) almonds, nibbed, or walnuts, crushed

50 g (2 oz) white breadcrumbs

1 small egg

SAUCE

2 tablespoons canned apricots in their own juice, mashed

about 150 ml (¼ pint) pure orange juice

1 tablespoon cornflour

Pig's Feet Crubeens with Michael Kelly's Sauce

Crubeens are a country dish which used to be a great favourite, accompanied by brown soda bread and pints of stout. The 'Grunter's Club' at Listowel always served them after the races and some pubs still serve them regularly. Usually the hind feet of the pig are used, as there is more meat on them than on the trotters.

The country method is to boil them in water with an onion, a carrot, some herbs and seasoning for about 2 hours. They can then be eaten either warm from the pot, or cold, taken up in the fingers and chewed, rather as one eats corn on the cob. A modern refinement is to split the foot in two, take out the bones, let it get cold, brush it with mustard, roll it in beaten egg and then in breadcrumbs, and either fry or grill it on both sides. Serve the crubeens with Michael Kelly's sauce below.

ALLOW 2 PER PERSON

Michael Kelly's Sauce

1 tablespoon brown sugar

1 teaspoon each dry mustard powder and freshly ground black pepper

2 tablespoons garlic vinegar

1 cup melted butter

Michael Kelly, born in Cork c. 1790, was an Irish composer who became director of music at the Theatre Royal, Drury Lane, in 1822.

This sauce can be served with crubeens (pig's feet), calf's head, boiled tongue or tripe.

Mix together the brown sugar, mustard powder and freshly ground black pepper, and stir in the garlic vinegar. Blend, then gradually mix with the melted butter.

Dublin Coddle

Combining two of the earliest Irish foods, this has been a favourite dish since the eighteenth century. It is said to have been much liked by Dean Swift.

Bring to the boil 1 litre (1 ¾ pints) of water and drop in the bacon and sausages, cut into large chunks. Cook for 5 minutes and drain, reserving the liquid. Put the meat into a large saucepan or ovenproof dish, mix with the sliced onions and potatoes, season well, and add about half the parsley. Add enough of the reserved stock to barely cover, lay greased paper on top, then a lid and either simmer gently or cook in a low oven at 150°C/300°F/gas mark 2 for about 1 ½ hours until the liquid has very much reduced and everything is cooked but not mushy. Garnish with the remaining parsley and serve hot with soda bread and Guinness.

SERVES 4–6

8 thick slices ham or bacon

8 large pork sausages

4 large onions, sliced

900 g (2 lb) potatoes, peeled and sliced

salt and pepper

4 tablespoons parsley, chopped

Liver Stroganoff

450 g (1 lb) liver
seasoned flour
4 tablespoons oil
2 large-sized onions, sliced
225 g (8 oz) mushrooms, sliced
salt and pepper
small carton natural yoghurt, or half yoghurt and half thick cream
pinch paprika
2 tablespoons parsley, chopped

Chicken, lamb or veal liver can be used in this recipe.

Cut the liver into fine strips and roll in seasoned flour. Heat up the oil and sauté the sliced onions until soft and golden but not brown; take out and put onto a dish. Add some fresh oil and lightly fry the sliced mushrooms, seasoning to taste. When ready, mix the mushrooms with the onions in the dish. Wipe out the pan with kitchen paper, add fresh oil, allow to heat and cook the liver quickly in it. Pour off any excess oil and add the mushroom and onion mixture, stirring well. Add a small carton of natural yoghurt (or the half yoghurt and half cream), season to taste and heat up but do not reboil. Garnish with a sprinkling of paprika and chopped parsley before serving with either rice or potatoes.

SERVES 4

VARIATION: Liver is very good, fried as usual, then the oil drained away and a little made mustard added to the pan juices and finally the plain yoghurt. Or use the onions and omit the mushrooms; whichever way is used, it is a good dish.

Farmhouse Terrine

Mince the belly of pork with the liver, but cut the drained boiling bacon into small cubes, seeing that all gristle, skin and bone are removed. Put the rashers on a flat surface and run the back of a thick knife over them, holding securely at one end so that they stretch considerably. Line the dish with the rashers, crosswise, and let the ends hang over the sides. Beat the egg yolks and mix with the meat mixture, garlic, rosemary and nutmeg. Season well and add the sherry. Put a layer on the bottom of the dish, then add the bacon cubes and cover again with the minced meats. Bring the bacon ends over the top and finally arrange the bay leaves over that.

Cover with foil and a lid, then stand the dish in another larger one, half filled with hot water. Bake in a moderate oven 180°C/350°F/gas mark 4 for about 1 ½ hours. Take from the oven, let it get cold, then cover with fresh foil and weight it for several hours (cans of food will do if you haven't got a flat weight). Serve cut into thick slices with bread or toast.

SERVES 6–8

VARIATION: Use rabbit, chicken or veal, or a mixture, instead of the boiling bacon.

450 g (1 lb) belly of pork

225 g (8 oz) boiling bacon, lean, soaked

450 g (1 lb) ox liver

pinch chopped rosemary

2 bay leaves

about 6 strips streaky bacon

1 garlic clove, crushed

salt and ground pepper

1 teaspoon nutmeg

2 egg yolks

3–4 tablespoons sherry or, better still, brandy

Devilled Kidneys

A good luncheon or supper dish. Mutton kidneys are the best for this method.

Trim and skin the kidneys, then halve them and remove the gristly white centre. Brush with oil and grill on both sides until they are well browned outside but still pink in the middle; this should take about 7 minutes. Meanwhile, mix together all the other ingredients in a basin. Just before serving, spread the mixture over the kidneys and heat for literally 1 minute under the grill.

ALLOW 2–3 KIDNEYS PER PERSON

6 kidneys

2 teaspoons Worcestershire sauce

2 teaspoons mushroom ketchup

110 g (4 oz) butter or margarine

2 teaspoons dry mustard

white pepper

oil for brushing

pinch each cayenne and salt

parsley to garnish

Liver Paté

Mince the liver very finely, and mix in the garlic and herbs. Season well, then add the beaten egg yolk and finally the stock or wine. Put into a greased dish, cover with foil or greased paper, then stand the dish in another larger one, half filled with hot water. Bake in a moderate oven for 1 ½ hours. Let it get cold before turning out or attempting to serve it. (It is better to leave it overnight.) Serve with slices of toast.

SERVES 2–4

450 g (1 lb) ox liver

1 egg yolk, beaten

½ wine glass red wine or equivalent stock

pinch powdered marjoram

2 cloves crushed garlic, optional, or use ½ small onion, finely minced

1 level tablespoon chopped parsley

salt and pepper

FISH

'To my mind [fish] is
the harassed housewife's
dream, for usually it comes
already prepared by the
fishmonger, and unless it
is a huge fish it takes very
little time to cook.'

Baked Salmon

1 salmon, about 2 kg
(4 ½ lb), cleaned and descaled

two sprigs parsley

3 heaped tablespoons butter

salt and freshly ground
white pepper

150 ml (¼ pint) dry white
wine or dry cider

300 ml (½ pint) double cream

juice of 1 lemon

Butter and cream figure extensively in Irish cooking, and both are used in making this delicious dish.

Trim the tail off the fish and put the parsley inside the cleaned gullet. Rub a little of the butter in an ovenproof dish and put in the fish; dot the rest over the salmon. Season, then pour the wine or cider around the dish, cover with foil and bake at 180°C/350°F/gas mark 4 for about 15 minutes to the half kilo (pound). After half an hour, take from the oven and baste slightly, then pour the cream over the fish, cover and put back in the oven to finish cooking.

When cooked, take from the oven, remove the skin and any side bones or fins. Put in a warmed serving dish and keep hot. Reduce the sauce on top of the stove, stirring all the time, add the lemon juice and taste for seasoning. Pour some sauce over the fish and serve the rest separately.

SERVES 8

Cod with Cockles

This is a traditional Galway dish made with a young codling, but it can be made with any white fish. Cockles are also used a great deal in counties Mayo and Donegal. Clams or mussels may be used instead, but if using mussels, chopped fennel should replace the thyme.

First discard any open cockles, then scrub the closed ones well. Put into a saucepan, barely cover with water, cover with a lid and put onto the stove. When the liquid boils, shake the pan for a minute or two and then take off the lid. Strain, reserving the juice, and when the cockles are cool enough, shell them.

Meanwhile, put the codling into a well buttered ovenproof dish and season well with salt, pepper and the thyme. Put the partly cooked potatoes and onions around the fish, and pour the cockles and the strained cockle juice over. Melt the rest of the butter and pour over, cover with foil or buttered paper and bake at 200°C/400°F/gas mark 6 for 20–25 minutes. Scatter the chopped parsley over the fish and serve with the lemon.

SERVES 4

24 cockles
1 kg (2 ¼ lb) codling
4 heaped tablespoons butter
salt and pepper
1 sprig fresh thyme or ½ teaspoon dried thyme
12 new potatoes, parboiled
6 small onions, parboiled
1 tablespoon parsley, chopped
lemon wedges to garnish

Fish Pie

450 g (1 lb) smoked cod or
haddock, or any fish or
fish combination

450 ml (¾ pint) milk

1 rounded tablespoon cornflour

2 tablespoons parsley, chopped

few drops of tabasco

200 g (7 oz) can tomatoes,
drained, or equivalent amount
fresh tomatoes, peeled,
chopped and drained

50 g (2 oz) grated cheese

450 g (1 lb) mashed,
cooked potatoes

butter

This can be extremely good and it is a pity the title is not
more attractive, although names such as 'fisherman's pie' are
now being used. The amount of seasoning depends on what
fish is used. Smoked fish is excellent, but if a plain fish is used
then more seasoning will be needed. Some grated cheese
added to the sauce is a simple but good idea. A mixture of
fish is pleasant and, when available, prawns or other shellfish
added will turn it into a very good meal.

Poach the fish in milk to cover, then remove the fish. Strain
and put the liquid back into the pan. Remove any skin or
bones from the fish. Cream the cornflour with a little of the
milk and add the rest to the pan. Bring to the boil, then
add the creamed cornflour, stirring all the time to avoid any
lumps.

Add the fish, parsley, tabasco and tomatoes, and mix
well, then add half the cheese. Put the mixture into an
ovenproof dish. Cover with mashed potatoes, scatter the
remaining cheese over the top and dot with butter. Bake at
200°C/400°F/gas mark 6 for about 35 minutes or until the
top is peaking brown.

SERVES 4–6

Kedgeree

Originally an Indian dish called *Khicharhi* which consisted of a mixture of rice, lentils, onion, spices, lime or lemon, butterfat and fish. It is good done as below.

Cook the rice until just tender, then drain well and stir gently with a fork. Cook the soaked fish, or drain the canned fish and break it into flakes. Then hard-boil the eggs for 10 minutes only and run under cold water. Shell and cut into quarters.

Mix all these ingredients together, adding most of the butter and using the rest to butter an ovenproof dish. Put the mixture into the dish together with the spices and season very well. Finally, pour over the cream and bake at 200°C/400°F/ gas mark 6 for about 20 minutes, or until hot through but not crisp on top. (This can be made ahead of time, but do not add the cream until just before cooking.) Sometimes I serve it with wedges of lemon and a little more melted butter poured over the top.

SERVES 4

350 g (12 oz) long-grain rice or brown rice, cooked

450 g (1 lb) smoked fish, soaked, or tinned salmon or tuna, drained

2 hard-boiled eggs

½ teaspoon each ground coriander and curry powder

25 g (1 oz) butter

2–3 tablespoons cream

salt and pepper

tabasco or cayenne pepper

Plaice Lahori

4 large plaice fillets

oil or melted butter

lemon wedges, to garnish

MARINADE

2 tablespoons onion,
finely minced

juice of 1 lemon

¼ teaspoon ground coriander
or 2 teaspoons fresh

pinch each powdered garlic
and turmeric

stem chopped green ginger or
¼ teaspoon ground ginger

pulp of 2 ripe tomatoes, no skin

salt and pepper

A great favourite of mine, but you do need large plaice, not those wafer-thin, tasteless little things you see most often. Actually, I have also made it with dogfish and monkfish fillets, and it was delicious, but it was cooked longer. (See also Chicken Lahori, page 25.)

Take the 4 large fish fillets and score with a sharp knife if very thick. Mix the marinade ingredients together, pounding well, then pour over the fish and leave for about 2 hours. Line a grilling pan with foil and brush over with oil or melted butter and turn on the grill. Let it get quite hot with the pan underneath so that the foil gets hot, but do not let the oil brown.

Lift the fish and marinade gently on and grill at medium level for about 7 minutes, or until the fish is cooked through. The heat of the foil at the bottom will cook the underneath. Serve with brown rice and green beans.

SERVES 4

Skate with Brown Butter

4 centre cuts skate (or ray)

175 g (6 oz) butter, melted

2 tablespoons capers

1 lemon cut in wedges

Choose the thick centre cut of the skate (or ray) if possible, although this is a good fish in all its cuts. There are no bones, just cartilage, which makes it popular with children. Also, it improves with keeping for a few days as it is a game fish. On the Scottish islands, it was liked quite 'high' and to this end was often earth-dried, that is put under sods of earth for a few days.

Poach the fish in enough salted water to barely cover for about 20 minutes, turning it halfway through cooking. Lift out and keep warm on a hot dish. Meanwhile, heat the butter until foaming and then let it go on cooking until it becomes a pale brown, but do not let it become too dark. Add the capers and some of the caper liquid, and as soon as the capers are heated through, pour over the fish and serve with the lemon wedges.

SERVES 4

Herb-stuffed Trout Wrapped in Lettuce

This is an exquisite way of cooking whole fish; it also looks very attractive. The fish should be a minimum weight of 700 g (1 ½ lb) after cleaning, and for a party several fish should be cooked.

First make the stuffing by mixing all ingredients together and reserve. Then take the largest lettuce leaves that are undamaged, about 10 or 12. Blanch them by pouring boiling salted water over them and then pat dry.

See that the centre backbone is taken out of the fish (you can ask the fishmonger to do this for you), then stuff the fish with the stuffing. Have ready a shallow, long ovenproof dish well buttered and scatter with the onion or shallots, then season. Season the outside of the fish and wrap it entirely in the lettuce leaves. Place in the buttered dish, dribble the Vermouth and wine over, dot with butter, cover with buttered paper or foil and bake at 220°C/425°F/gas mark 7 for 15 minutes. Baste with the juices and cook again for the same length of time, still covered.

When cooked, lift out carefully with fish slices, keep hot and pour the juices into a small saucepan. Reduce a little by rapid boiling, then add the cream and a few little nuts of butter to give it a glaze. Either pour over or serve separately.

SERVES 2

1 trout or bass, about 700 g (1 ½ lb) when cleaned

10–12 outer leaves lettuce

salt and white pepper

50 g (2 oz) butter

2 tablespoons finely chopped onion or shallot

2 tablespoons each dry Vermouth and white wine

a little cream

STUFFING

110 g (4 oz) spinach, cooked, finely squeezed and chopped

3 tablespoons dry fresh breadcrumbs

about 2 teaspoons melted butter

2 tablespoons mixed parsley, tarragon and sorrel, chopped

1 small egg, beaten

Mackerel with Gooseberries

Grilled or fried mackerel served with a gooseberry sauce is well known and very good, as the acid gooseberry cuts the oily flavour of the fish. But it can also be baked with gooseberries in cider.

Top and tail the gooseberries, then mix well with the sugar and nutmeg. Put a layer of mackerel in an ovenproof dish and cover with the gooseberries, then put the remaining layer of mackerel over the top. Sprinkle with salt and pour the cider over. Cover and bake at 180°C/350°F/gas mark 4 for about 40 minutes.

SERVES 2–4

4 mackerel, cleaned and filleted

225 g (8 oz) gooseberries

2 tablespoons brown sugar or to taste

pinch ground nutmeg

salt

approx. 300 ml (½ pint) cider

Devilled Crab

700 g (1 ½ lb) crabmeat

300 ml (½ pint) whipping cream

1 teaspoon anchovy essence (available in good speciality food stores)

2 teaspoons mushroom ketchup (available in good speciality food stores)

2 teaspoons Worcestershire sauce

¼ teaspoon dry mustard

salt and pepper

cayenne pepper

8 green olives, stoned and chopped

1 lemon, cut into wedges

This was a famous dish in Ireland in the eighteenth and nineteenth centuries. It was also used as a savoury.

Put the crabmeat in an ovenproof dish. Whip the cream until firm and gradually add all the remaining ingredients, except the lemon wedges, whisking gently to keep the sauce thick. Spread the sauce evenly over the top of the crabs and bake high up in a preheated oven at 200°C/400°C/gas mark 6 for about 15 minutes. Serve with the wedges of lemon.

SERVES 6

Mussels Stuffed with Garlic

'Rí sea diúilicíní ach ria tualaigh sea bairnigh.'
('Mussels are the food of kings, limpets are the food of peasants.')

450–700 g (1–1 ½ lb) shelled cooked mussels or 2 ¼ litres (4 pints) if bought in the shells

110 g (4 oz) butter

2 large cloves garlic, crushed

juice of ½ large lemon

salt and pepper

1 tablespoon parsley, finely chopped

lemon wedges to garnish

Mussels have always been eaten in Ireland, usually by coastal dwellers, but they were also hawked around the streets of Drogheda and of course Dublin, as evidenced in the old song about Molly Malone who 'wheeled her wheelbarrow through streets broad and narrow'.

Today the mussels of Wexford are particularly large and succulent, a commercial mussel farm having been established there, but there are also many fine mussels in other parts of Ireland. This is a modern recipe given to me by the Irish Aquaculture Association.

Put the mussels into an ovenproof dish. In a saucepan, heat the butter until just melted, add the garlic, then the lemon juice, salt and pepper and chopped parsley. Mix well and when amalgamated and very hot, pour gently over the mussels. Run the dish under a hot grill until peaking brown.

SERVES 4

Dublin Bay Prawns in Batter

40 Dublin Bay prawns

110 g (4 oz) plain flour

¼ teaspoon salt

150 ml (¼ pint) tepid water
or beer

1 tablespoon oil, preferably olive

oil for deep-frying

1 large egg white

This is a very popular way of serving Dublin Bay prawns
which are often, alas, designated on the menu as 'scampi'
which, although a first cousin, is an Adriatic shellfish; this is
the Norway lobster.

The batters can vary. Sometimes it is simply a matter
of dipping the whole prawns in beaten egg and then in
breadcrumbs. The following batter is extremely light and
crispy and very good for fritters or for small pieces of chunky
white fish, scallops and so on. Using beer in place of water for
this batter will give an even lighter batter with a good flavour.

Mix the flour and salt with the oil, then add the water or beer
and beat well. The batter will be quite thick, but it should be
smooth. Cover and set aside until needed (do not chill). Just
before the batter is needed and as the oil for deep-frying is
heating up, beat the egg white until stiff and carefully fold it
into the batter. When the oil is very hot, drop in the battered
pieces of fish and cook on both sides until golden.

SERVES 4–6

Dublin Lawyer

This is a traditional method of serving lobster which is extremely delicious. If possible make this dish with a raw lobster, that is one which has been killed just before cooking by plunging a sharp instrument into the cross on the head. However, a lightly cooked lobster can be used and will still be extremely good. This dish can be served with boiled rice if liked.

1 fresh lobster, about 1 kg (2 ¼ lb), cut in two down the centre

3 heaped tablespoons butter

4 tablespoons Irish whiskey

150 ml (¼ pint) cream

salt and pepper

Remove all the meat from the lobster, including the claws, and retain the shells for serving. Cut the meat into chunks. Heat the butter until foaming and quickly sauté the lobster chunks in it until just cooked but not coloured. Warm the whiskey slightly, then pour over the lobster and set fire to it. Add the cream, mix with the pan juices and taste for seasoning. Put back into the half shells and serve hot.

SERVES 2

Risotto di Scampi

450 g (1 lb) fresh Dublin
Bay prawns, shells on

1 small garlic clove

1 tablespoon parsley,
freshly chopped

110 ml (3 ½ fl oz) oil or a
mixture of oil and butter

450 g (1 lb) Arborio rice

100 ml (3 ½ fl oz) dry white
wine

freshly ground pepper and salt

1 tablespoon butter

grated Parmesan

A favourite Venetian speciality is Risotto di Scampi.
Depending on the size of the prawns, you should allow
between 4 or 6 per person.

Rinse the prawns, then cook in 1.7 litres (3 pints) of
simmering water for 3–4 minutes until cooked through. Cool
a little before removing the shells. Then return the shells to
simmer in the cooking liquor until needed while you prepare
this dish.

Chop the garlic very finely and sauté lightly in the oil, using
a wooden spoon. Add the washed and drained rice, then
turn and stir so that every grain is coated with oil. Pour in
the wine, turn up the heat and let it evaporate. Season with
pepper and a little salt. Strain the cooking liquor to use as
stock. Then add about 1 cup of stock to the pan, stirring
while cooking over a moderate heat until the rice absorbs the
liquid.

Add a little more stock at intervals as needed until the rice
is tender but firm. When cooked, it should be creamy and
smooth but not glutinous. Add the prawns and then the
parsley and the butter to give it a shine. Mix gently and serve.
A little grated Parmesan is stirred into the risotto just before
serving.

SERVES ABOUT 4

*VARIATIONS: You do not have to use Dublin Bay prawns if they are too
expensive or difficult to find. The smaller prawn can be used, or chunks of a
firm fish, or indeed cooked mussels, or a mixture. If using the fish, then it should
be turned in oil or butter before adding to the rice.*

Potted Crab

450 g (1 lb) crabmeat
juice of 1 lemon
110 g (4 oz) butter
¼ teaspoon ground mace
salt and pepper
150 g (5 oz) clarified butter

This will keep for about a week, but once the butter cover has been opened up, it should all be eaten.

Mash the crabmeat finely. Pound it with the lemon juice, butter, mace, salt and pepper. Put into a pot, pressing down well into all the corners, then cover thickly with the clarified butter. Chill until ready to serve.

SERVES 4

Scallops Meunière

If using the large scallops cut into 2.5 cm (1 in) chunks, but leave the Queens whole. Put into a saucepan with the bay leaves and barely cover with water, bring to the boil and simmer for 10 minutes if large; 5 if Queens. Drain, but reserve the liquid and let it reduce slightly so that it is about half the volume.

Melt the butter and add the drained scallops, letting them brown slightly and cook thoroughly. Season, then add the sherry, juice of lemon and just enough stock to make a good sauce. Boil up for about five minutes and serve garnished with chopped parsley.

SERVES 4–6

12 large scallops or 4 dozen (48) Queens

50 g (2 oz) butter or 4 tablespoons olive oil

juice of 1 lemon

2 bay leaves

1 small glass sherry

salt and pepper

parsley to garnish

EGGS AND CHEESE

'The egg is versatile, practical and
cheap: it is also, as Oscar Wilde said, an
adventure, for each one can be treated
in so many ways for a savoury, sweet or
even a liquid dish.'

Convent Eggs

4 eggs

2 tablespoons butter

1 medium-sized onion, sliced

1 tablespoon flour

300 ml (½ pint) milk

½ teaspoon salt

¼ teaspoon pepper

grated cheese or chopped herbs, optional

This recipe, which I have adapted very slightly for modern use, comes from Soyer's *A Shilling Cookery for the People* of 1859, a book that circulated in many parts of Ireland after Soyer came over to help provide edible food for the famine victims. My copy originally belonged to my aunt in Co. Clare and was much used by her.

Put the eggs into cold water, bring to the boil and boil for 10 minutes, then put the eggs into cold water again. When cool, peel and cut across into six pieces each. Heat the butter and lightly fry the onion in it until soft but not coloured. Add the flour and mix well, then add the milk, stirring until it forms a nice white sauce; add the salt and pepper. Add the eggs, toss, and when they are hot through, serve on toast. Grated cheese or chopped herbs can also be added.

SERVES 4

Broad Bean or Nettle Purée
with Sausages and Eggs

450 g (1 lb) broad beans
or nettles

2 tablespoons melted butter

salt and pepper

6 eggs, scrambled

8 sausages

4 slices bread

2 tablespoons butter

This is my grandmother's recipe which she used to make
when her broad beans had become too old to eat without
being skinned. Nettles in place of beans are delicious in spring
and very good for you. Gather the nettles before the end of
May, wearing gloves, and do not gather them from any verge
that might have been chemically sprayed.

Cook the broad beans, drain and then sieve them, or put
through a vegetable mill so that the skins are left behind. If
using nettles, cook and chop the tops. Put into a saucepan
with the melted butter and salt and pepper. Mix well and
keep warm. Grill the sausages and keep hot. Toast the 4 slices
of bread and butter the toast slices. Spoon the broad bean
purée over, dividing it among the toast slices, and keep warm.
Scramble the eggs very lightly, that is take them off while
the top is still creamy, and spoon over the bean purée on the
toast. Add the grilled sausages, two to a portion.

SERVES 4

Omelette Arnold Bennett

This is a great favourite of mine. It is a delicious meal for two people, and a fresh, crunchy salad is pleasant to eat afterwards.

Flake the cooked fish and mix with the grated cheese, seasoning to taste. Beat the eggs and heat the butter until foaming in a thick, heavy pan, but do not let the butter brown. Pour in the eggs and mix up with an egg slice so that they form a little mound in the middle, then tip the pan so that the uncooked egg runs over any bare spaces. Do not let it get too cooked; it should still be quite runny when you put the fish and cheese mixture over the top evenly. Take from the heat after 1 minute, pour the cream over evenly and put under a hot grill for 2–3 minutes so that the top is golden and bubbling.

This omelette is slid from the pan to the plate, not folded up, and it should be put onto a hot dish or 2 hot plates.

SERVES 2

175 g (6 oz) cooked smoked haddock or cod

6 eggs

2 tablespoons thick cream

2 tablespoons grated hard cheese

1 tablespoon butter

freshly ground pepper

Irish Omelette

4 eggs
1 tablespoon butter
squeeze of lemon juice
1 large cooked potato
salt and pepper

This might come as a surprise to some people, but I found this recipe in an eighteenth-century manuscript, spelt 'amulet' (maybe it was considered lucky to eat it), and it is extremely good and filling.

Mash the potato very well and separate the yolks from the whites of the eggs. Add the yolks to the potato, mixing very well, then season to taste and add the lemon juice. Heat the pan with butter. Whisk the whites stiffly, stir into the mixture, and then add to the heated pan. Cook the bottom until golden, then put under a hot grill to finish the top. Originally the top was finished with a 'brander' which was a heated disc of metal, often used in conjunction with the girdle or griddle, for baking.

SERVES 2

VARIATIONS: I often add a tablespoon of chopped herbs or a very small amount of grated cheese to the above mixture.

In Scandinavia an omelette is invariably baked in a greased dish in the oven (as for a puffy omelette) and 4 eggs would have about a 150 ml (¼ pint) cream beaten into them.

In Portugal an omelette is a very odd bird, consisting of beaten eggs usually combined with cooked brains, or chopped cooked meats, all mixed together so that the eggs coat the meat. It is quite dry, served in a small heap, but not unpleasant to taste. It is, however, rather a shock if you are expecting a golden, bubbling plateful of food like a tortilla or a French omelette, for it resembles an overcooked piperade and defies all the things I have written about above.

Le Pounti

This is a good egg dish which comes from the mountains of the Auvergne. It is like a sort of meat loaf soufflé if you can imagine such a thing.

Set the oven to 180°C/350°F/gas mark 4. Chop the bacon, ham, onion, garlic, parsley and spinach, and mix together. Sift the flour into a bowl and make a well in the middle, then gradually add the milk. Whisk in the eggs to make a smooth batter and season to taste. Mix this batter into the bacon mixture.

Butter a 1.5 litre (2 ½ pint) ovenproof dish and pour the mixture in. Bake for 50–60 minutes at the above temperature until set. Serve hot or warm, cut into wedges like a cake. It is very good with a green vegetable such as peas or beans, or a mixture with sweetcorn.

SERVES ABOUT 6

110 g (4 oz) bacon, chopped

110 g (4 oz) cooked ham, chopped

1 medium-sized onion, chopped

1 garlic clove

110 g (4 oz) spinach

salt and pepper

3 tablespoons parsley, chopped

100 g (3 ½ oz) flour

600 ml (scant pint) milk

4 eggs

Basic Pancake Mixture

150 g (5 oz) flour

pinch of salt, or sugar for sweet pancakes

1 large beaten egg, or 1 medium and 1 egg yolk

300 ml (½ pint) milk

2 teaspoons cold water

1 teaspoon oil for frying

French pancake batter always has the egg and egg yolk in it, and a French chef gave me a good tip for making pancakes creamy yet crisp. It is to heat up about a heaped teaspoon of butter in the pan and then to tip it into the batter; it also prevents the pancakes getting rubbery in storage.

Sift the flour and salt into a basin. Add the egg and mix well, then gradually add the milk, beating all the time. Finally, add about 2 teaspoons of cold water and beat again with a whisk. Leave for about half an hour, then beat again before using.

The pan must be a heavy, flat-bottomed one and should be preheated before cooking. When it is hot, add about 1 teaspoon of oil or margarine and run it evenly all over the pan. Then add about 1 large tablespoon batter and *immediately* tilt the pan so that it spreads evenly: about a 15 cm (6 in) diameter is handy for turning. Either flip or turn with an egg slice when it is speckled underneath, then cook the other side the same way.

MAKES ABOUT 10 SMALL PANCAKES

Sweet Pancakes

Sweet pancakes can vary from the simple sprinkle of sugar with a squeeze of lemon to the more elaborate but delicious Crêpes Suzette, which are cold pancakes folded into four, then reheated in butter, with liqueurs such as Cointreau, brandy, Irish Mist and so on. They are excellent and a pleasant sweet to prepare at the table over a spirit lamp.

I think fruit purées are delicious, even an ordinary fruit such as apple puréed and mixed with apricot jam with a little dash of sherry or a liqueur. This is also very good for the gâteau-type of pancake dish. Or fill with the purée and then flambé with whiskey, Irish Mist or brandy.

Savoury Sauces

Do not make these sauces too thick and stodgy: if the pancake is filled with minced chicken or fish, then mix some through this and reserve the rest for pouring over the top either when reheating or at the table. Cheese, mushroom or fresh tomato sauce is very good, and a white sauce with just a hint of curry powder in it is good with chicken, but if it is to be poured, then see that it is a pouring sauce. The quantities are: 25 g (1 oz) each flour and butter, and 450–600 ml (¾–1 pint) milk, all stirred very well to avoid lumps.

Savoury Fillings

Almost anything can be used so long as it is either chopped very finely or minced, with the exception of cheese fillings. The best way to make these is to make a *thick* white sauce and then to add the grated cheese of your choice to it. Crumbled Irish blue cheese is very good, as is a grated hard cheese such as Cheddar.

Oatmeal Bacon Pancakes

110 g (4 oz) flour
25 g (1 oz) oatmeal
about 240 ml (1 cup)
milk or buttermilk
salt
1 egg, beaten
8 bacon rashers
mustard

Selina Newcomen of Mosstown, Co. Longford, 1717, gives a very lavish recipe for pancakes which is interesting historically:

Eight Egg yolks and whites, half a pint of flower blended smooth with a pint of Milk, a naggin of Brandy, a little Nutmeg and Ginger. Two ounces of melted Butter – Salt and Sugar to your taste. Mix them well together very little Butter will answer for frying them.

And underneath is written: Pan Cakes.

One Doz Eggs to a pint of flower and a quart of Milk makes a great deal more and I find answer as well.

These pancakes have a nutty flavour and are delicious for breakfast.

Sift the dry ingredients, then add the egg and enough milk or buttermilk to make a batter-like thick cream. Fry the bacon rashers and drain, then make a large pancake, pouring the batter over the entire bottom of the pan. Cook on one side, toss over, spread with a little mustard if liked, then add the bacon and fold over. Make the rest of the batter into pancakes the same way.

MAKES 2 VERY LARGE PANCAKES OR 4 SMALLER ONES

Wicklow Pancakes

4–6 eggs, depending on size

600 ml (1 pint) milk

110 g (4 oz) fresh breadcrumbs

1 tablespoon parsley, chopped

pinch chopped thyme

2 tablespoons chopped chives or scallions

salt and pepper

2 tablespoons butter

This is a traditional Wicklow dish. Although it is called a 'pancake', it is more like a substantial omelette.

Beat the eggs lightly, then add the milk, breadcrumbs, herbs and seasoning, and mix well. Heat one tablespoon of the butter in a pan until foaming, then pour in the mixture and cook over a low flame until brown underneath and just set on the top. Put under the grill to finish. Serve cut into wedges with a knob of butter on each portion.

SERVES 4

Croque Monsieur

Croque Monsieur is popular in France and one of my favourites.

Beat the egg with the milk and season with pepper, then dip the bread quickly in this mixture, turning over as soon as it is coated so that it does not absorb too much liquid. Heat up the fat or oil and slice the cheese into four, then turn on the grill to heat up. Fry the bread in the oil on both sides until just golden, then put onto the grilling rack. Lay a slice of ham or bacon on top, then the cheese. Put under the hot grill until the cheese is bubbling.

SERVES 2

VARIATIONS: Vegetarians or people not wishing to eat meat can substitute the ham for cooked spinach; drained sweetcorn; baked beans; peeled, sliced tomatoes; or a drained tin of tuna fish. Cover with cheese as above and grill.

4 thickish slices crustless bread

1 egg

4 tablespoons milk

4 slices cooked ham or equivalent bacon rashers, lean, cooked

110 g (4 oz) hard cheese such as Cheddar or Cheshire

50 g (2 oz) butter, margarine or oil

pepper

Eggs Fitzmaurice

8 eggs, lightly poached in advance

2 tablespoons butter

2 tablespoons flour

1 heaped tablespoon grated hard cheese, preferably Parmesan

300 ml (½ pint) milk

salt and pepper

cayenne pepper

50 g (2 oz) breadcrumbs

lard or oil for deep-frying

several fresh sprigs of parsley

This unusual egg dish was often served by a very elderly cousin of mine, who must have been born in the 1870s. She got the recipe from her grandmother, Geraldine Fitzmaurice, who was born in 1831. It makes a most delectable first course.

It is important that the eggs be poached some time before they are needed, as they must be quite cold, and drained well. Trim them neatly if they were not cooked in a poacher.

Heat the butter and when foaming add the flour and stir well. Cook for about a minute, then gradually add the milk, stirring all the time until the mixture is thick and smooth. Add the cheese and stir until it melts thoroughly, then add the salt, pepper and cayenne. Beat well, then leave for a few moments to cool slightly. Heat the lard or oil for deep-frying. Dip the eggs in the sauce and then into the breadcrumbs, and lower into the hot fat. Fry until golden brown, then put the eggs into a warmed dish and keep warm while you deep-fry the parsley sprigs for about 20 seconds. Garnish the dish with the parsley sprigs.

SERVES 4

Welsh Rarebit

Welsh Rarebit takes a lot of beating if made in the proper way.

Add the flour, mustard, Worcestershire, butter and pepper to the grated cheese. Mix well, then add the beer to moisten, but do not make it too wet. Stir over a gentle heat until melted, then stop stirring and lift the pan from the heat, twirling the mixture round the saucepan. Let it cool slightly, when it will be quite a thick paste. (This paste can be stored in a cold place and used later on if required.) Toast *one side only* of thick bread and spread the paste on the untoasted side, then brown under a hot grill.

SERVES 2

VARIATION: Sweet white wine can also be used instead of beer and gives a subtle, good flavour; Guinness makes it quite strong to taste, so it may be advisable to use only half the quantity.

225 g (8 oz) grated Cheshire, Cheddar or Gloucester cheese

1 level tablespoon flour

½ level teaspoon dry mustard pepper

1 tablespoon Worcestershire sauce

4 tablespoons (approx.) beer or Guinness

1 level tablespoon butter or margarine

pepper

VEGETABLES

'Vegetables, being as expensive as they are,
should be treated with the respect they deserve
and cooked in ways which will give them plenty
of flavour and variety.'

Artichoke Pie

450 g (1 lb) Jerusalem artichokes

1 tablespoon butter or margarine

1 tablespoon flour

300 ml (½ pint) warm milk

1 small bunch seedless or
seeded white grapes

10 dates, stoned and halved

1 hard-boiled egg

pinch mace

salt and pepper

milk to glaze

PASTRY

225 g (8 oz) flour

110 g (4 oz) butter or margarine

approx. 4 tablespoons cold water

pinch salt

First make the pastry by working the butter into the flour and salt with your fingers until it resembles coarse breadcrumbs, then add the water and mix to a smooth, firm paste. Turn out onto a floured board and roll into a ball. Keep in a cold place until wanted. (Packaged pastry can be used if preferred.)

Peel the artichokes and boil in salted water for about 10 minutes or until they are almost cooked, then drain them. Heat the butter, stir in the flour and add the warm milk, stirring all the time until smooth. Simmer gently for a few minutes and see that it is not too thick; if so, add a little more milk (or a little white wine). Add the artichokes, grapes, dates and mace to the sauce and season well. Put this mixture into a pie dish, slice the hard-boiled egg over the top, then moisten the edges of the pie dish and roll out the pastry to the required size. Press down the edges, brush lightly with milk and bake in a moderate oven at 180°C/350°F/gas mark 4 for 30 minutes.

SERVES 4–6

Creamed Cabbage

This dish was a favourite in Limerick and Tipperary when I was young, but it is undoubtedly very much older.

Trim the cabbage and remove the tough stalk, then cut into eighths and blanch for 5 minutes in boiling salted water. Drain very well and then cut into thin strips. Heat the butter, stir in the flour and cook for 1 minute, then gradually add the milk and nutmeg, stirring well to avoid lumps. Add the cabbage and bring back to the boil, seasoning to taste. Cover and cook gently for 15 minutes, stirring from time to time. Serve the cabbage, still a little crunchy, in the creamy sauce.

SERVES 4–6

1 white or young green cabbage, about 1 kg (2 ¼ lb)

2 tablespoons butter

2 level tablespoons flour

pinch grated nutmeg

600 ml (1 pint) creamy milk or thin cream

salt and pepper

Beetroot in Orange Sauce

Excellent as a first course or with cold meats or poultry.

Combine all ingredients except the cornflour and yoghurt or cream, seeing that the beets are thinly sliced. Boil and then add the creamed cornflour, stirring well to avoid lumps. Simmer very gently for about 5 minutes. Serve with a blob of yoghurt or cream over the top of each portion.

SERVES ABOUT 4

450 g (1 lb) cold cooked beets (various types of beets can be used)

2 tablespoons honey

300 ml (½ pint) beet juice

1 dessertspoon cornflour

2 tablespoons plain yoghurt or cream

1 teaspoon finely grated orange peel

pinch crushed cardamom

salt and pepper

Broad Beans Theodora

900 g (2 lb) young broad beans, shelled

225 g (8 oz) bacon in one piece, soaked

reserved water from the cooked beans

25 g (1 oz) butter or margarine

salt and pepper

3 garlic cloves, optional

300 ml (½ pint) creamy milk or cream

2 tablespoons parsley, chopped

25 g (1 oz) flour

This is a way of my own which satisfies my love of broad beans, and it can be made ahead of time and reheated.

Cook the shelled beans in boiling water with very little salt, then strain but reserve the stock. Boil the soaked bacon in one piece for about half an hour, then take out and chop into cubes. Heat the butter, add the flour, and when well mixed, add 150 ml (¼ pint) of bean water, stirring well, and finally the milk. Heat and stir until smooth. Add the seasoning and combine with the bacon, garlic and parsley. Transfer all the ingredients to a casserole and cook for 20 minutes at 200°C/400°F/gas mark 6.

SERVES 4–6

VARIATIONS: Leftover pork or bacon, or sausages first browned, can be used in this recipe, too.

Colcannon

450 g (1 lb) kale or cabbage

450 g (1 lb) potatoes

2 small leeks or green onion tops

about 150 ml (¼ pint) milk or cream

pinch mace

salt and pepper

about 110 g (4 oz) butter, melted

This is traditionally eaten in Ireland at Hallowe'en or All Hallows' Day, 31 October. Until quite recently this was a fast day, when no meat was eaten. The name is from *cal ceann fhionn* – white-headed cabbage. Colcannon should correctly be made with cooked, finely chopped kale (a member of the cabbage family), but it is also made with white cabbage.

An interesting version is the Irish Folklore Commission's, which gives it as mashed potatoes mixed with onions, butter and milk with a boiled white cabbage in the centre. Colcannon at Hallowe'en used to contain a plain gold ring, a sixpence, a thimble or a button; the ring meant marriage within the year for the person who found it, the sixpence meant wealth, the thimble spinsterhood and the button bachelorhood.

If using the kale, strip from the stalks, or likewise remove the stump of cabbage, before cooking in boiling salted water until tender but not overcooked. Drain very well and chop finely. Meanwhile, cook the potatoes and chop the leeks or onion tops, then simmer in milk or cream to cover for about 7 minutes. Drain the potatoes, season and mash well, then stir in the cooked leeks or onions tops and milk, adding a little more milk if needed.

Finally, blend in the finely chopped kale or cabbage – a blender or food processor is ideal for this. Add the mace and taste for seasoning. Heat the entire mixture gently, then pile into a warmed dish. Make a small well in the centre and pour in the melted butter.

SERVES ABOUT 6

Carrot Pie or Pudding

This eighteenth-century recipe from Sara Power's handwritten book of 1746 gives a good idea of how carrots were used as a sweet dish.

Take half a pound of butter, the yolk of 10 eggs, half a pound of powder sugar, and one spoonful of orange flavour water, beat your eggs well and beat your butter either to cream or melt it in Oyle, then take well colour'd carrots, boyle, and pare them well, so mix and beat all together, put it in a dish and do the brim with puff paste, bake it an hour, you must pound the carrots.

It makes a delicious first course or last course.

I make a sort of flan like this: mix together the carrots, butter, egg yolks (or two whole eggs), sugar to taste, orange flower water and creamy milk or thin cream. The mixture is then poured into a 22.5–25 cm (9–10-in) flan case lined with flaky pastry (see page 260) and baked for 30 minutes.

SERVES 4

350 g (12 oz) mashed, cooked carrots

2 tablespoons butter

4 egg yolks or 2 whole eggs

sugar to taste

1 teaspoon orange flower water (obtainable from chemists)

about 1 cup creamy milk or thin cream

Parsnip Cakes

These are excellent with pork, ham, bacon and sausages.

Peel and slice the parsnips, then boil in salted water until tender. Drain and mash well. Add the flour, mace, melted butter, salt and pepper, then form into 8 flat round cakes to give 2 per serving. Dip into the beaten egg, then into the breadcrumbs and fry in hot oil until brown on both sides.

SERVES ABOUT 4

450 g (1 lb) parsnips
2 large tablespoons flour
pinch ground mace
2 tablespoons melted butter
salt and pepper
1 large egg, beaten
8 rounded tablespoons breadcrumbs
oil for frying

Fadge

1 kg (2 ¼ lb) freshly
mashed, cooked potatoes

2 tablespoons melted
butter or bacon fat

4 tablespoons flour, or more

salt

Fadge is the Northern Irish name for this potato cake dish,
usually served with bacon and eggs for breakfast. The cakes
can be stored in a tin for reuse.

Add the butter or bacon fat to the mashed potato and then
work in the flour and mix well. (You may need a little more
flour if the potatoes are not very floury.) Add salt to taste,
then turn out onto a floured surface. Roll out to a 1 cm
(½ in) thickness, then cut into large rounds or triangles. Have
ready a heated, lightly greased griddle or heavy pan. Prick the
potato cakes on both sides and fry for about 3 minutes on
each side.

MAKES ABOUT 12 CAKES

Mushoshi

An Armenian brown lentil salad with apricots and nuts which is delightful.

First cook the lentils. If you have a pressure-cooker, they will take 25 minutes, barely covered in water. Otherwise cook in water until tender, which can take up to an hour. Make certain you do not over-cook them. When ready, salt to taste. Stir in the onion, apricot and walnuts, and cook for a further 15 minutes, then strain the mixture and leave to cool. Put into a serving bowl.

In a small bowl, mix together the dressing ingredients, except the parsley. Pour over the dressing, mixing well, adding the parsley last. Toss well and serve.

SERVES ABOUT 3

VARIATION: Beans can be used instead of lentils if liked.

175 g (6 oz) brown lentils, soaked

1 small onion, chopped

75 g (3 oz) dried apricots, chopped

50 g (2 oz) walnuts, chopped

DRESSING

3 tablespoons olive oil

1 ½ tablespoons lemon juice

salt and black pepper

2 tablespoons parsley, chopped

Sweet and Sour Onions

450 g (1 lb) onions, sliced
6 tablespoons oil
salt and pepper
3 tablespoons white wine vinegar
3 tablespoons castor sugar

These are very good with fried or grilled liver, kidneys, steak, chops or sausages.

Heat the oil, and when hot, add the sliced onions and cook gently with the lid on until soft. Drain off the oil and season lightly to taste. Then add the sugar, mixing well, and finally the vinegar. Heat up and simmer for 5–7 minutes or until it becomes syrupy. Small pickling onions can be used but should be left whole and boiled first, then put into the vinegar and sugar.

SERVES 4

Peperonata

An Italian dish that can be served as a vegetable with roasts or grills, as an omelette filling, with cold meats, or as a first course.

Heat the oil and butter, and fry the finely sliced onion until soft but not coloured. Add the strips of peppers, season, cover and simmer for 15 minutes. Finally, add the tomatoes and garlic, season again and cook gently for about half an hour.

SERVES 4

VARIATIONS: Season the original mixture very well, then put into an ovenproof dish and beat in 2 eggs very thoroughly. On top break 4 eggs very carefully so that the yolks are intact, pour over a dribble of oil and bake in a hot oven at 200°C/400°F/gas mark 6 for about 20 minutes. This makes a good luncheon or supper dish. Without the top eggs, it is a kind of piperade and is very good served with dry toast as a first course, or it can be served with boiled rice or pasta.

1 tablespoon olive oil

1 tablespoon butter

1 large onion, finely sliced

4 sweet peppers, cut in strips

6 ripe peeled tomatoes or 425 g (15 oz) can

2 garlic cloves

salt and pepper

Peas with Lettuce

900 g (2 lb) shelled peas
6 spring onions, chopped
10 outer lettuce leaves
1 tablespoon parsley, chopped
3 tablespoons butter
pinch salt and sugar
8 tablespoons water

Petit pois à la Française.

Cut the lettuce into strips and place in a saucepan. Add all the other ingredients except the sugar, then cover and simmer for about 20 minutes or until the peas are cooked. About 3 tablespoons of liquid should be left in the saucepan. Taste and add a pinch of sugar if necessary: some peas are sweeter than others, so the seasoning should be adjusted to personal taste. Do not strain but serve in the sauce.

SERVES 6

Pickled Samphire

Rock samphire (*Crithmum maritimum*) can be found very often growing on the tops or sides of cliffs. It is a small, fleshy-leafed branching plant which has an unusual flavour. It figures a lot in old cookery manuscripts, sometimes chopped and put into a cream sauce but mainly pickled. It can also be steamed until tender and served with melted butter. The taste – slightly resinous – is one that I find attractive.

Pick the tops and buds of the samphire and pack in a wide-mouthed jar. A few tiny pickling onions can be added – they will acquire a most delicate flavour. Make a spiced vinegar of white vinegar, pickling spices, bay leaf, allspice berries and sugar. Bring to the boil, then cool, strain and pour over the samphire buds until quite covered. Tie down and store in a cool place. This pickle will last for some time. It can also be preserved in lightly salted water.

MAKES A JAR OF PICKLED SAMPHIRE

bunch samphire

pickling onions, optional

1 litre (1 ¾ pints) white vinegar

1 heaped teaspoon pickling spices

1 bay leaf

2 allspice berries

about 1 tablespoon sugar

Porri al Forno

12 large leeks

2 rashers bacon

300 ml (½ pint) milk or cream

1 or 2 eggs, depending on size, beaten

1 tablespoon flour

50 g (2 oz) grated cheese

salt, pepper and nutmeg

300 ml (½ pint) leek stock

Porri al Forno, leeks baked in the oven, is a popular Italian method.

Trim the leeks and slice in half lengthwise, then simmer in water for 10 minutes. Drain well, reserving 300 ml (½ pint) of the liquid. Chop the bacon into small pieces and fry until the fat comes out. Sprinkle with the flour, mixing well, then add the milk or cream and the leek stock, stirring all the time to avoid lumps. Add the nutmeg and season to taste, then add the well beaten egg(s), beating well off the heat. Add the leeks and turn into an ovenproof dish. Cover with the grated cheese and bake in a hot oven for about 10–15 minutes or until the top is brown.

SERVES 2–4

Potatoes à la Dauphinoise

This is the French version of scalloped potatoes and you will need the finest, waxiest potatoes to make this dish at its optimum. It is served with meats, poultry or fish, but it is almost a meal on its own.

First butter an ovenproof dish thickly. Fill it with alternate layers of sliced potatoes (double the thickness of a penny) and the grated cheese, seasoning each layer with salt, pepper and nutmeg. Beat together the egg and creamy milk, such as jersey, or cream. When the dish is almost full, pour over the egg and cream, and finish with a good sprinkling of cheese. Cook in a moderate oven at 180°C/350°F/gas mark 4 until the potatoes are done and the top crisp and golden. This normally takes about 1 hour, but some potatoes can take longer.

SERVES 6–8

900 g (2 lb) potatoes, sliced

110 g (4 oz) grated cheese, Blarney, Gruyère or a really hard Cheddar

salt and pepper

nutmeg

1 egg

scant 300 ml (½ pint) creamy milk or cream

little butter

Ratatouille

1 medium-sized marrow,
peeled and seeded

1 large onion

4 tablespoons milk

salt and pepper

4 large tomatoes

150 ml (¼ pint) oil

1 large clove garlic

½ sliced green pepper if available

Usually made with courgettes and aubergine, both of which, if available, can be used in this recipe. With the addition of chopped ham, chicken, tongue or grated cheese, this can be served as a light meal.

Peel and slice all the vegetables, then layer in an ovenproof casserole, seasoning well between each layer. Pour over the oil and the milk, and cover and bake in a moderate oven for barely 1 hour. If liked, a thick sprinkling of grated cheese can be put on top, in which case remove the lid for the last 10 minutes to let it brown.

SERVES 4

DESSERTS AND PUDDINGS

'All Irish people have a very sweet
tooth and will spend hours making
elaborate puddings and decorating
cakes for the delectation of themselves
and their families.'

Black Cap Pudding

½ tablespoon butter

110 g (4 oz) blackcurrants, cleaned, topped and tailed

squeeze of lemon juice

3 heaped tablespoons sugar

150 g (5 oz) fresh breadcrumbs

75 g (3 oz) flour

2 large eggs, beaten

300 ml (½ pint) milk

a little butter

The blackcurrant is a valuable fruit full of vitamin C which grows freely in Ireland. This pudding was originally made with black raspberries – a very dark-red raspberry hardly ever seen these days except in gardens. Nowadays it is made with blackcurrants.

Butter a 1-litre (2-pint) pudding basin. Put the blackcurrants in a saucepan with the lemon juice and 2 of the tablespoons of sugar. Cook gently for about 5 minutes and then transfer to the basin.

Sift the flour into a bowl, add the breadcrumbs and the final tablespoon of sugar, and mix well. Make a well in the middle and add the beaten eggs and mix. Finally, add the milk and beat well. Leave to stand for about 15 minutes. Pour over the blackcurrants, cover and tie down, then steam for 2–2 ½ hours. Turn out by reversing the basin so that the 'black cap' covers the pudding. Serve with cream.

SERVES 4–6

October Cobbler

450 g (1 lb) blackberries,
elderberries, damsons and plums

1 tablespoon lemon juice

50 g (2 oz) butter

3 heaped tablespoons sugar

175 g (6 oz) self-raising flour

pinch salt

110 g (4 oz) butter

3 tablespoons milk

This pudding is to be made with a mixture of autumn fruits gathered early in the month of October.

Clean the fruits and put with the sugar and lemon juice in a buttered pie dish, then dot with butter. Sift the flour with the salt and rub the remaining butter in. Mix in the milk to make a firm but elastic dough. Roll out and put roughly over the fruit, pricking all over with a fork. Bake at 200°C/400°F/gas mark 6 for 30 minutes. Serve hot with cream.

SERVES 4–6

Blancmange

This was a great pudding for all of the nineteenth century and half of the twentieth, called a 'shape' in Ireland. Other flavourings that can be used instead of vanilla are chocolate, coconut, coffee or almond essence, or rum. If the finished pudding, when cold, is studded all over with blanched almond halves, angelica and currants, to make a 'face', the result will be the pudding called 'hedgehog'.

Mix the cornflour, sugar and salt with the milk, stirring until smooth, then add to the scalded milk and stir well again. Put into the top of a double boiler (bain-marie) over hot water and cook for 15 minutes, stirring constantly until the mixture thickens. Take off the heat and stir a little until it cools slightly. Wet a mould. Add to the mixture the vanilla, and the beaten egg whites if using, stir and pour into the wetted mould. Leave in a cold place to set.

SERVES 4–6

3 tablespoons cornflour

110 g (4 oz) sugar

pinch salt

3 tablespoons milk

600 ml (1 pint) milk, scalded

1 teaspoon vanilla

2 egg whites, stiffly beaten, optional

Bread and Butter Pudding

½ tablespoon butter

6 thin slices bread, crusts removed, buttered

110 g (4 oz) sultanas and raisins (include chopped peel if liked)

75 g (3 oz) brown sugar

3 eggs

850 ml (1 ½ pints) milk

A pinch of mixed spice or a teaspoon of rum essence is sometimes added to the sugar in this recipe.

Butter a 1-litre (2-pint) pie dish. Cut the bread into squares or triangles and arrange half in the dish. Scatter the sultana mixture over the bread, add about two-thirds of the sugar, then put the rest of the bread on top. Beat the eggs with about half the remaining sugar, add the milk and mix, then pour over the contents of the pie dish; it should about half-fill the dish. Leave to stand for half an hour or longer. Sprinkle with the final amount of sugar and bake at 180°C/350°F/gas mark 4 for about an hour or until the custard is set. It can be eaten hot or cold.

SERVES 4–6

Carrageen Jelly

Soak the carrageen in water for a few hours, then rinse well and drain. Put in a pan with the water and simmer for about 20 minutes, then strain and discard the carrageen. Add the lemon juice, sugar and finally the sherry to the strained liquid, and stir. Wet a mould, pour in the liquid and put in a cold place to set.

15 g (½ oz) carrageen
450 ml (1 pint) water
2 teaspoons lemon juice
sugar to taste
small wine glass sweet sherry

SERVES 4

Christmas Pudding 1

450 g (1 lb) demerara sugar

450 g (1 lb) fresh breadcrumbs

75 g (3 oz) ground almonds

175 g (6 oz) chopped
candied peel

75 g (3 oz) glacé cherries

450 g (1 lb) currants

275 g (10 oz) raisins

275 g (10 oz) sultanas

1 medium-sized carrot, grated

juice and grated rind of 1 lemon

juice and grated rind of 1 orange

1 teaspoon mixed spices

7 eggs

300 ml (½ pint) Guinness

2 tablespoons flour

150 ml (¼ pint) whiskey,
brandy or rum

This rich Christmas pudding is comparatively recent in the Irish cuisine. Formerly a simple boiled fruit pudding was sometimes served, but since the beginning of the twentieth century the Christmas pudding has become traditional. An old lady of my acquaintance remembers young domestic science teachers going around the country and teaching countrywomen how to make them. Previously they had already become popular among owners of large houses, who had travelled. They should be made not later than the first week in November, to give them time to mature, but they can be made earlier, as they will keep for a year.

Mix the sugar, breadcrumbs and almonds in a large bowl. Add the candied peel, cherries, currants, raisins, sultanas and grated carrot. Mix well. Make a well in the middle and add the grated lemon and orange rinds and both juices, then add the mixed spices and mix again. Beat the eggs with the Guinness and add them gradually, alternately adding a little flour each time. Stir very well. Finally, add the spirits that you are using and mix again.

At this point it is traditional to get all the family to stir and to make a wish. Also, a small coin is usually wrapped up and added to the mixture for luck.

Butter the bowl (or bowls) well and fill with the mixture to within 2.5 cm (1 in) of the top. Cover with greaseproof paper, then either a lid or foil, or a cloth, and tie down. Steam over boiling water for 7 hours or a little longer. Lift out and uncover the pudding(s) and let the steam out. Leave to cool.

Cover again when cool and store in a cool, dark place until 25 December. On Christmas Day, steam the pudding for a further 1 ½ hours before serving, decorated with a piece of berried holly. At the table, pour over a warm ladleful of Irish whiskey and set it alight. If possible it should be eaten at once – it is considered good luck to eat it while the blue flame is still burning. Serve with brandy sauce or brandy butter.

MAKES THREE 1-KILO (2-POUND) PUDDINGS OR ONE VERY LARGE ONE

Dublin Rock

This rich and decorative pudding of the nineteenth century was often decorated with angelica, blanched split almonds and branches of maidenhair fern or other plants, to look like plants growing out from a rocky hillside.

Cream the butter with the sugar, then add the lightly whipped cream. Fold in the ground almonds and mix very gently so as to avoid oiling. Add the orange flower water and the brandy, and finally fold in the stiffly beaten egg whites. Put the mixture into a dish and place in the coldest part of the refrigerator to harden. Then break into rough pieces and pile these, pyramid fashion, on a glass dish, and decorate as imaginatively as desired.

SERVES 4

110 g (4 oz) unsalted butter

110 g (4 oz) fine sugar

300 ml (½ pint) thick cream, partially whipped

225 g (8 oz) ground almonds

few drops of orange flower water (obtainable from chemists)

1 tablespoon brandy

2 egg whites, stiffly beaten

Lemon Soufflé

This is a very fresh, non-fattening soufflé which can also be made with orange, lime and grapefruit instead of lemon.

Combine the egg yolks, sugar and lemon rind and juice, and mix very well with a wooden spoon. Dissolve the gelatine in 150 ml (¼ pint) water in a saucepan, stirring over a low heat for a minute or two. Pour into the lemon mixture in a steady stream, stirring from time to time to blend well. Leave for about half an hour until it begins to set. Beat the egg whites stiffly. With a metal spoon, add the beaten egg whites, getting right down to the bottom of the mixture. Pour into serving dishes and chill to set.

SERVES 4–6

4 large eggs, separated
175 g (6 oz) sugar
finely grated rind of 1 lemon
3–4 tablespoons lemon juice
15 g (½ oz) powdered gelatine

Marmalade Fruit Pudding

4 tablespoons marmalade

175 g (6 oz) butter

175 g (6 oz) sugar

175 g (6 oz) self-raising flour

2 large eggs, beaten

finely grated rind of 1 lemon

½ tablespoon butter for greasing

75 g (3 oz) chopped fruit, dates, figs or chopped peel

This can be made with jam or fruit preserve, or golden syrup, instead of marmalade if preferred. It should be served with custard or cream. If made in small individual moulds, they are called 'castle puddings'.

Cream the butter and sugar until light. Combine a spoonful of flour with a little of the beaten egg and beat into the mixture; repeat and continue until all the flour and eggs are added. Add the finely grated lemon rind and chopped fruit, then mix well.

Butter a 450–700 g (1–1 ½ lb) pudding basin and put the marmalade in the bottom, then pour the mixture on top, making sure it does not come within 2.5 cm (1 in) of the top. Cover with greaseproof paper and either tie down or add a lid. Steam over boiling water for 1 ½–2 hours. Turn out carefully onto a warmed plate.

SERVES 4–6

Spotted Dog

An account of convent life in Co. Limerick in the 1870s gives the favourite puddings as jam tart, dog-in-a-blanket and spotted dog. I do not have a dog-in-a-blanket recipe, but here is one for spotted dog.

Sift the flour into a basin, add the breadcrumbs, suet, currants, sultanas and lemon rind. Mix with the egg and a little water to a soft dough. Roll out on a floured surface to a rectangle about 1 cm (½ in) thick. Spread butter along one end, then roll up like a Swiss roll and press the edges together. Wrap loosely to allow for expansion in a cloth or foil and tie at each end. Lower into boiling water and simmer for 2–2 ½ hours. Unwrap and put onto a serving dish, slice and serve hot either with custard or (as I remember with pleasure) with golden syrup slightly warmed.

SERVES 4–6

110 g (4 oz) self-raising flour
110 g (4 oz) fresh breadcrumbs
110 g (4 oz) shredded suet
110 g (4 oz) currants
2 heaped tablespoons sultanas
grated rind of 1 lemon
1 egg
2 tablespoons softened butter
custard or warmed golden syrup

Sussex Pond Pudding

225 g (8 oz) self-raising flour

110 g (4 oz) grated suet or margarine

approx. 150 ml (¼ pint) milk and water, mixed

175 g (6 oz) butter (do not use margarine), cut in small pieces

175 g (6 oz) soft, light brown sugar or castor

1 large lemon, washed and dried

This is just about my favourite in the winter.

Grease a 1.1 litre (2 pint) pudding basin well. Mix the flour and suet or margarine together very well, then add enough milk and water to make a soft dough. Turn onto a floured board and knead gently for a few minutes. Cut off a quarter of the dough and set aside for the lid. Roll out the remaining dough to fit the sides and bottom of the basin.

Mix the butter with the sugar. (If liked, 2 tablespoons honey can be substituted for 50 g (2 oz) sugar.) Prick the lemon all over with a thin skewer and stand upright in the middle of the basin, then pack the butter and sugar mixture around it. Roll out the remaining piece of dough to make a lid, dampen the edges and press on well. Lay a pleated, buttered piece of foil over the top and tie in place with string.

Then either boil, with water just coming up to the brim, or steam for 3–4 hours. Check that the water does not dry up; if it does, add more boiling water. To serve, put a large warmed dish over the top and quickly turn upside down. When cut, a 'pond' of butter and sugary liquid makes a moat around the pudding. Make certain that everyone gets a piece of the lemon, too.

SERVES 4–6

Burnt Oranges

... fine oranges
Well roasted, with sugar and wine ...
JONATHAN SWIFT, 1723

4 large oranges

150 ml (¼ pint) sweet white wine

1 teaspoon butter

4 teaspoons fine sugar

300 ml (½ pint) freshly squeezed orange juice

4 heaped tablespoons sugar

2 tablespoons whiskey, warmed

Peel the oranges thinly, then with a sharp knife carefully remove as much of the pith and white skin as possible, keeping the oranges intact. Cut the thin peel into fine strips and cover with the wine. Put the oranges into an ovenproof dish. Put a little butter on top of each one, pressing it down gently, then sprinkle each one with a teaspoon of fine sugar. Put into a 200°C/400°F/gas mark 4 oven for 10 minutes or longer until the sugar caramelises.

Meanwhile, mix the orange juice with the sugar in a saucepan and bring to the boil. Lower the heat and cook until it gets syrupy, without stirring. Add the orange peel and wine mixture and bring to the boil again, then cook rapidly to reduce and thicken slightly.

Take the oranges from the oven. If not fully browned, put under a moderate grill for a few minutes. Pour over the warmed whiskey and set alight over heat. As the flames die down, add the orange syrup and let simmer for about 2 minutes. Serve at once or it can be served cold.

SERVES 4

Rhubarb Charlotte

Heat the butter and toss the crumbs in to combine, shaking the pan. Spread a thin layer of the mixture over the bottom and sides of a 1-litre (2-pint) soufflé dish, reserving some. Put in half the rhubarb pieces. Mix together the brown sugar, spices and grated orange rind, and sprinkle about half over the rhubarb. Then repeat the layers. Top with the reserved crumbs.

Combine the golden syrup with the lemon or orange juice and 2 tablespoons of water, beat well and pour over. Cover and bake at 200°C/400°F/gas mark 6 for 30 minutes, then uncover and cook for 10 minutes more. Serve with cream.

SERVES 4

2 heaped tablespoons butter, melted

175 g (6 oz) fresh breadcrumbs

450 g (1 lb) rhubarb, cleaned and cut in 2.5 cm (1 in) pieces

50 g (2 oz) brown sugar

pinch ground ginger

pinch cinnamon

pinch nutmeg

grated rind of 1 orange

2 tablespoons golden syrup

2 teaspoons lemon or orange juice

Blackberry Amber

450 g (1 lb) blackberries

a little water

75 g (3 oz) and 50 g (2 oz) castor sugar

1 egg yolk

4 tablespoons milk

3–4 sponge cakes or double sponge fingers

1 egg white

This is a very good way to serve blackberries as the top of the dessert is both soft and crisp.

Cook the blackberries, water and enough sugar to sweeten, then put the fruit and some, but not all, of the juice into a buttered pie dish. Beat the egg yolk with the milk, cut the sponge cakes in half and soak in the egg and milk mixture.

When the sponge cakes have absorbed the egg and milk, lay them over the blackberries to cover. Preheat the oven to 180°C/350°F/gas mark 4 and cook for about 20 minutes or until the top is golden brown. Meanwhile, whip up the egg white, add the castor sugar, take out the amber (the fruit and sponges) from the oven, and spread the egg mixture over the top.

Turn the oven down to 140°C/275°F/gas mark 1 and put back in oven, leaving for about 15 minutes or until the top is amber-brown. Serve hot with cream.

SERVES ABOUT 4

VARIATION: Blackberry and apple can also be used.

Pear Sponge Cake

110 g (4 oz) butter

110 g (4 oz) sugar

2 eggs

450 g (1 lb) ripe pears
(cookers or eaters)

110 g (4 oz) self-raising
flour, sifted

whipped cream

A deliciously light cake-pudding, to be eaten warm or cold.

Cream the butter and sugar until light, then add the eggs, one at a time, beating each one in well. Peel, core and slice the pears. Fold the flour into the sugar, butter and egg mixture. Stir in the pear slices. Line a 20 cm (7 ½ in) cake tin, preferably one with a removable base, and spoon in the mixture. Bake at 190°C/375°F/gas mark 5 for 30–40 minutes or until a skewer comes out clean. Serve with whipped cream.

SERVES 4–6

Italian Chocolate Dolce

This is a kind of crunchy, rich chocolate mousse and small portions are advised if you do not want to overdo it.

Put the chocolate and butter into a bowl and stand this over a saucepan of hot water until both melt. Separate the eggs and beat the yolks with the sugar until pale. Crush the biscuits roughly and slowly stir in the yolks and sugar. When that is well mixed, add the chocolate mixture. Mix well again, then cool slightly.

Meanwhile, whisk the egg whites and fold in with a metal spoon. Pour into a serving bowl or individual dishes and chill for at least 8 hours. Before serving, whip the cream stiffly and spread over the top, then sprinkle with the grated chocolate. Keep cool until serving time.

SERVES 4–6

75 g (3 oz) plain chocolate, broken up

175 g (6 oz) butter, cut in small pieces

3 eggs, separated

50 g (2 oz) dark chocolate, grated

75 g (3 oz) castor sugar

150 g (5 oz) plain sweet biscuits, slightly crushed

150 ml (¼ pint) double cream

Apple Layer Meringue

Arrange the apple in a buttered ovenproof dish in layers with the brown sugar, mace, glacé fruit and lemon. When the dish is full, the last layer being apples, cover with foil and bake in a moderate oven at 180°C/350°F/gas mark 4 for about 40 minutes or until the apples are quite soft.

Take out of the oven, remove the foil and cover with the thin bread and butter, buttered side down. Put back in the oven for about 10 minutes or until the top is crisp and brown. Add the castor sugar to the beaten egg whites and spread this meringue over the top, sprinkle with a little more sugar and put into a cool oven just until the meringue is set and golden brown. It is best eaten cold.

SERVES 4–6

700 g (1 ½ lb) eating apples, peeled, cored and quartered

175 g (6 oz) brown sugar

1 lemon, thinly sliced, pips removed

2 tablespoons glacé fruit, sliced

4 egg whites, stiffly beaten

8 tablespoons castor sugar

4 very thin slices of bread and butter

pinch mace

Apricot or Peach Shortcake

SHORTCAKE

225 g (8 oz) plain flour

3 level teaspoons baking powder

3 tablespoons castor sugar

50 g (2 oz) soft butter

2 egg yolks

150 ml (¼ pint) milk

FILLING

450 g (1 lb) can apricots or peach halves, or use fresh fruit

3 tablespoons honey

300 ml (½ pint) double cream

a little butter

Other fruit such as fresh strawberries can be used.

First make the shortcake by sifting the flour and baking powder, then adding sugar, into a bowl. Work in the butter, beat the egg yolks and milk together, and add gradually until there is a soft but pliable dough. Knead lightly. Roll out a shape into a 12 cm (7–8 in) round (or 4 individual ones). Put onto a greased baking sheet and bake for 15–20 minutes in a preheated oven at 212°C/425°F/gas mark 7. Cool on a rack covered with a cloth.

To prepare the filling, strain the apricots or peaches and mix with 1 spoonful of honey. Whip the cream and add a little more honey to sweeten. Chop up most of the fruit, leaving about 8 to garnish, and add to the cream mixture. Then carefully split the warm shortcake, butter the bottom layer lightly and spread with the rest of the honey. Spread most of the cream mixture over and put the other layer on top. Garnish the top with the remaining cream and fruit.

SERVES 6

Trifle or Typsy Cake

This delicious pudding, which is an old Christmas speciality, has regrettably been allowed to run down over the years, owing to the use of packaged custard powder, instead of homemade, and the inclusion of canned fruits and jelly. When well made, it takes a lot of beating.

Split the sponge cakes in two, spread the bottoms with the jam and put back the tops. Arrange in a large glass dish, cover with the macaroons and ratafias, pour the sherry over and sprinkle with the almonds and lemon rind.

To make the custard, beat the egg yolks, then gradually mix in the hot milk and stir over a very low heat or in the top of a double boiler (bain-marie) until it runs off the back of a wooden spoon in ribbons. Never allow to boil, just to thicken slightly. Take off the heat and stir in the sugar. Let the custard cool a little, then pour over the contents of the glass dish. Leave to cool.

To finish, cover the top with the whipped cream and decorate with cherries, almonds and angelica.

SERVES 6–8

6 trifle sponge cakes

raspberry or strawberry jam

6 tiny macaroons

10 ratafia biscuits

300 ml (½ pint) medium sherry

grated rind of ½ lemon

25 g (1 oz) blanched shredded almonds

CUSTARD

4 egg yolks

600 ml (1 pint) milk, heated

2 tablespoons sugar

300 ml (½ pint) double cream, whipped

glacé cherries, split almonds and angelica for decoration

Linzertorte

PASTRY

225 g (8 oz) flour

1 good pinch each ground
cloves and ground cinnamon

pinch salt

1 grated lemon rind

110 g (4 oz) soft margarine

75 g (3 oz) castor sugar

50 g (2 oz) ground almonds

1 large egg

FILLING

350 g (12 oz) red, black or
white currants or jam

110 g (4 oz) raspberries

75 g (3 oz) castor sugar

This is an Austrian tart using soft fruits such as raspberries or strawberries and redcurrants. Jam can be used if fruits are not available.

Preheat the oven to 190°C/375°F/gas mark 5. Sift the flour, spices and salt, then add the grated lemon rind. Cut the margarine into small pieces and with the fingertips rub into the flour. Stir in the sugar and ground almonds. Lightly beat the egg, then using a fork, mix the egg into the dry ingredients, wrap in greaseproof paper and chill for 1 hour.

On a floured surface, roll out the pastry into a circle and carefully line a lightly greased 23 cm (9 in) fluted flan dish. It is short pastry so needs gentle handling. Trim the edges, then roll up, seeing that you have enough for lattice strips. Re-roll this and cut into 10 × 1.25 cm (½ in) strips.

Wash the currants, take off the stalks and mix with the raspberries, then put in the flan and sprinkle with the sugar. Lay lattice strips over and leave for 15 minutes before baking. Bake on centre shelf for 35–40 minutes until golden brown. Serve hot or cold with cream. This freezes well.

SERVES 6

French Apple Tart

PASTRY

200 g (7 oz) plain flour

110 g (4 oz) butter or margarine

1 egg yolk

25 g (1 oz) castor sugar

pinch salt

FILLING

450 g (1 lb) small cooking apples

110 g (4 oz) castor sugar

2 large eggs or 3 small

150 ml (¼ pint) cream or jersey milk

This is creamy and excellent and needs no additions, and it is good served either hot or cold.

Sift the flour into a bowl, add the butter in small pieces and rub until it is like coarse breadcrumbs. Add the egg yolk, sugar and salt, and mix to a dough. Roll into a ball and chill for at least 30 minutes. Meanwhile, peel, core and halve the apples, then thinly slice without separating the slices. Roll out the pastry to fit a 23–25.5 cm (9–10 in) loose-based flan tin, arrange the apple slices on the pastry and bake this at 200°C/400°F/gas mark 6 for 20 minutes. The apples should be lightly cooked.

Beat the sugar with the eggs and cream, and pour over. Bake for a further 20–30 minutes until the creamy custard is set and slightly browned.

SERVES 4–6

Rhubarb Bakewell Tart

Make the pastry first, then chill it for at least half an hour. Preheat the oven to 200°C/400°F/gas mark 6.

Roll out the pastry to fit a 20 cm (8 in) flan tin and lightly prick over the bottom. Cream together the butter and sugar until light, then mix in the ground almonds and finally the beaten egg. Spread the strawberry jam over the bottom of the pastry, then add the rhubarb. Cover with the almond mixture, roll out the leftover pastry strips and criss-cross over the top, brushing with a little milk. Bake in the centre of the oven for 15 minutes, then lower heat to 180°C/350°F/gas mark 4 and continue cooking for another 15–20 minutes or until set and the pastry is golden brown. Serve warm or cold.

SERVES 6–8

375 g (13 oz) shortcrust pastry (see page 260)

2–3 tablespoons strawberry jam

350 g (12 oz) rhubarb, cut into 2.5 cm (1 in) pieces

50 g (2 oz) butter

110 g (4 oz) brown sugar

50 g (2 oz) ground almonds

1 egg, beaten

Blueberry Syllabub

225 g (8 oz) blueberries

50 g (2 oz) castor sugar

2 teaspoons lemon juice

300 ml (½ pint) cream for whipping

1 tablespoon brandy or sherry, optional

A simple yet delicious method.

Warm the blueberries with the sugar and lemon juice very gently, just enough to make the juices run, then rub through a sieve or mill. Whip the cream lightly and continue beating as you slowly add the blueberry juice mixture. Add the brandy if using. Pour into serving glasses and chill before serving.

SERVES 4–6

Café Liegeois

6 tablespoons vanilla or coffee
ice-cream

4 coffee cups strong,
sweetened black coffee

150 ml (¼ pint) whipped cream

4 teaspoons crushed ice

Put all ingredients, except the whipped cream, into a bowl
and stir well, or liquidise until the mixture is thick and
creamy. Pour into 4 tall glasses and top with whipped cream.
Chill so that it is semi-frozen and serve with sponge fingers.

SERVES 4

Treacle Sponge

Mix all the ingredients together well, but add the egg last.
Pour into a greased basin or dish, then cover and steam for 2
hours. Turn out to serve with custard, cream, more treacle or
golden syrup.

SERVES 4–6

175 g (6 oz) self-raising flour

110 g (4 oz) shredded suet

½ teaspoon ground ginger

150 ml (¼ pint) milk

110 g (4 oz) sugar

110 g (4 oz) treacle

1 egg

custard, cream, more
treacle or golden syrup

Gooseberry Fool

450 g (1 lb) gooseberries
(no need to top and tail if
you have a Mouli-mill)

75 g (3 oz) sugar, or to taste

a few heads of elderflower if
available

squeeze of lemon

2 egg whites, stiffly beaten

about 3 tablespoons thick cream

nuts, angelica, finely grated
lemon or orange rind to garnish

Very easy to do and quite delicious after a good meal on a
summer's evening.

Cook the gooseberries in very little water, about 3
tablespoons, with the sugar, and just as they are bursting, add
the elderflower heads and leave for about 5 minutes. Then
take out and put the gooseberries through a Mouli-mill.

Whip the egg whites until stiff and also thicken the cream a
little, but do not beat too much. Add a squeeze of lemon to
the gooseberries, then fold in the egg whites and finally the
cream.

Serve in glass bowls or stemmed glasses and garnish with
chopped nuts, strips of angelica, and finely grated orange or
lemon rind. Chill until serving. Little biscuits such as *langues
de chat* or boudoir biscuits are good to serve with this.

SERVES 6

Strawberry Mousse

This is my own recipe which is simple, good and not too rich.

Pick over the strawberries and mash or purée them. Then sieve the cheese, beat in the egg yolks and sugar, and add the strawberries. Dissolve the gelatine in the hot water, and when thoroughly dissolved and cool, add the cream, whisking until stiff. Fold this carefully into the strawberry mixture and pour into a 1.7 litre (3 pint) mould, lightly oiled and sprinkled with castor sugar (or use smaller individual moulds). Tie a paper collar around the top if you want it to stand impressively over the top of the dish and remove before serving. Chill until set.

SERVES 6–8

350 g (12 oz) strawberries

450 g (1 lb) cottage cheese

4 egg yolks

75 g (3 oz) castor sugar, or to taste

25 g (1 oz) gelatine

12 tablespoons very hot water

300 ml (½ pint) cream

VARIATION: *If liked, this mousse can be made without the strawberries; instead they can be served with it, having been sprinkled with a little orange liqueur or juice.*

Christmas Pudding 2

110 g (4 oz) plain or self-raising flour

2 teaspoons each cinnamon, mixed spice and nutmeg

350 g (12 oz) fresh breadcrumbs (bread not more than 2 days old)

50 g (2 oz) ground almonds

225 g (8 oz) brown sugar

1 carrot, grated

rind and juice of 1 orange and 1 lemon

225 g (8 oz) each sultanas, seedless raisins and currants

110 g (4 oz) chopped glacé cherries

175 g (6 oz) chopped mixed peel (the whole peel is the best)

225 g (8 oz) grated suet or butter, margarine or oil

300 ml (½ pint) Guinness

4 tablespoons rum, whiskey or brandy

5 eggs

Put the prepared fruit and all the dry ingredients into a large bowl and mix well. Make a well in the bowl and add the grated rind and juice of the orange and lemon and the grated carrot. Mix again. Beat the eggs and add gradually, stirring well. Finally, add the stout and spirit, mixing together very thoroughly. Add any charms or an old sixpence if available. Put into greased basins, cover with greaseproof paper and then tie a cloth over. (If necessary, they can be left overnight.)

Steam or boil with the water coming up to the rim for seven hours, topping up with water as it runs dry. When cooked, uncover and let the steam out. Do not be alarmed if they are not dark brown, this comes with age. Re-cover lightly with greaseproof paper and the following day tie up with clean cloths. Before serving, steam or reboil for 2 hours.

Puddings can also be cooked in the oven in the following way: put the puddings in a large tin three-quarters full of hot water, cover the puddings completely in foil and bake at 150°C/300°F/gas mark 2 for 6 hours.

MAKES TWO PUDDINGS OF 1.2 LITRE (2 PINT) SIZE

BREADS, BISCUITS AND CAKES

'An old country superstition is
to "nip the cake", that is, when a
cake is freshly baked a small piece is
broken off to avert bad luck. Children
sometimes overdo this custom!'

Apple Bread

225 g (8 oz) flour

175 g (6 oz) sugar

110 g (4 oz) butter

4 large cooking apples, peeled, cored and finely minced

1 egg, beaten

butter for spreading

This tea bread is pleasant served warm, sliced and with butter.

Combine the flour and sugar in a bowl and rub in the butter until the mixture becomes like coarse breadcrumbs. Add the minced apples and beaten egg, and mix well. Turn into a shallow 20 cm (8 in) baking tin and bake at 180°C/350°F/ gas mark 4 for about 40 minutes or until brown and cooked through. Cut into pieces and butter before serving.

SERVES 4–6

Boxty Cakes or Bread

Boxty on the griddle, Boxty in the pan,
If you don't get Boxty, you'll never get a man.

Boxty is traditional in the northern counties such as Cavan and Donegal, in the form of cakes, bread, dumplings, pancakes and puddings. Mr Patrick Gallagher, born in Cleendra, Donegal in 1873, recalled just before his death at the age of 92 that, when he was a child, boxty bread was often served instead of oat bread, with milk and salt, and called 'dippity'.

Peel the raw potatoes and then grate the peeled potatoes into a basin lined with a napkin or cloth. Wring tightly over the basin, catching the liquid. Put the wrung-out grated potatoes into another basin and spread with the cooked mashed potato. When the starch has sunk to the bottom of the raw potato liquid, pour off the top and add the starchy part to the potato mixture. Sift the flour with the baking powder, add to the mixture, mix well and season to taste. Add the melted butter or bacon fat and mix in. If the mixture seems too soft, add some milk gradually.

Turn out onto a floured surface and knead lightly, then shape into 4 flat, round cakes. Mark a cross on each one, to let them rise properly and so that they will divide into farls when cooked. Put onto a greased baking sheet and bake at 160°C/325°F/gas mark 3 for 30–40 minutes. Serve hot, split, and with butter.

MAKES 16 'FARLS' OR 4 CAKES

450 g (1 lb) raw potatoes

450 g (1 lb) freshly mashed cooked potatoes

450 g (1 lb) self-raising flour

2 teaspoons baking powder

salt and pepper

60 ml (2 fl oz) melted butter or bacon fat

about 150 ml (¼ pint) milk

Country Cheese Bread

225 g (8 oz) white flour

225 g (8 oz) wholemeal flour

1 level teaspoon salt

1 level teaspoon
bicarbonate of soda

1 heaped tablespoon butter

2 medium-sized onions,
grated or finely chopped

2 teaspoons mixed fresh
herbs or 1 teaspoon dried

2 tablespoons parsley, chopped

about 150 ml (¼ pint) milk

about 150 ml (¼ pint)
buttermilk or lemon juice

50 g (2 oz) finely grated cheese

Sift the flours, salt and soda into a bowl, then tip in the bran from the sieve. Rub in the butter and add the onion, herbs and parsley. Add enough milk and buttermilk or lemon juice to make a soft dough, only adding a bit at a time. Turn out and knead a little, then shape into a round of about 5 cm (2 in) thickness. With a floured knife mark the top into 8 wedge sections or farls and put onto a lightly floured baking sheet. Brush with milk and sprinkle the grated cheese all over the top. Bake in a preheated oven at 200°C/400°F/gas mark 6 for 35–40 minutes until done.

MAKES 8 'FARLS'

Apple and Oatmeal Cake

450 g (1 lb) cooking apples, peeled, cored and sliced

2 heaped tablespoons sugar, or to taste

½ teaspoon cinnamon

1 heaped tablespoon raisins

110 g (4 oz) butter

1 heaped tablespoon brown sugar

1 tablespoon honey

275 g (10 oz) medium oatmeal

grated rind of 1 lemon

2 large eggs, beaten

cream, optional

This is a layer cake full of fibre, which is good eaten either as a cake or as a pudding with cream.

Simmer the apples with the sugar and cinnamon until they form a purée. Add the raisins and leave to cool. Melt the butter, sugar and honey in a saucepan. Combine the oatmeal and finely grated lemon rind in a bowl. Pour the honey mixture over, then add the beaten eggs and mix all together very well. Divide this mixture in three. Press one third into a cake tin with a removable base, cover with half the apple mixture, then add another third of the oatmeal mixture, then apple, then oatmeal. Bake at 190°C/375°F/gas mark 5 for 30–35 minutes. Serve warm or cold with cream.

SERVES 6–8, DEPENDING ON APPETITES

Buttermilk Bread

This is a very traditional bread. For the recipe I am indebted to Honor Moore.

Stir the buttermilk into the oatmeal in a large bowl, then cover and leave for 12 hours. Mix and add the flour, soda, sugar or honey, and a little more buttermilk, enough to make a fairly stiff dough. Well grease two loaf tins and bake at 200°C/400°F/gas mark 6 for 45–55 minutes, but test before taking from the oven. Turn out and wrap in a tea towel to cool.

MAKES 2 LOAVES

about 750 ml (1 ¼ pints) buttermilk

225 g (8 oz) fine or medium oatmeal

225 g (8 oz) white flour or a mixture of white and wholemeal

1 teaspoon baking soda

1 teaspoon salt

2 tablespoons brown sugar or honey

Potato Yeast Rolls

110 g (4 oz) potatoes

25 g (1 oz) fresh yeast or
15 g (½ oz) dry yeast

50 g (2 oz) sugar

450 g (1 lb) white flour (warm
the flour in a warmed bowl if it
has been stored in a cool place)

1 teaspoon salt

50 g (2 oz) butter

150 ml (¼ pint) warmed milk

1 egg, beaten

milk for glazing

These are the lightest and most delicious rolls I have ever tasted. They freeze very well too.

Cook the potatoes in salted water and drain, reserving 2 tablespoons of the cooking liquid. Mash the potatoes very well or press through a fine sieve into a basin, then cover and keep warm. Cream the yeast in a bowl with the reserved tepid potato liquid and a spoonful of the sugar, and mix well as it froths up (if it does not froth, it is not satisfactory to use). Sift the flour into a large mixing bowl with 1 teaspoon salt and rub in the butter. Make a well in the centre and add the rest of the sugar and the mashed potatoes, mixing well. Add the tepid milk and 150 ml (¼ pint) water to the yeast liquid, mix and add to the mixing bowl, then beat in the beaten egg. Knead very well. Cover and leave in a warm place for about an hour, until doubled in size.

Turn out onto a floured surface and shape into rolls. Put the rolls onto a greased baking sheet, well spaced, to allow for rising. Cover and leave for 20 minutes. Brush with a little milk and bake at 220°C/425°F/gas mark 7 for 15–20 minutes.

MAKES ABOUT 16

Cheese Biscuits

This was a popular biscuit to make in the early years of the twentieth century, often served with consommé. It is a delicious biscuit to serve with drinks.

Work all the ingredients together on a slab with the hands until well mixed (do not add any water). Put onto a lightly floured surface and roll out fairly thinly. Cut into rounds about 4 cm (1 ½ in) across. Put onto greased baking sheets, well spaced, to allow for rising. Bake at 200°C/400°F/gas mark 6 for about 10 minutes. Serve the sooner the better within 24 hours.

MAKES ABOUT 8–10 BISCUITS

2 heaped tablespoons sifted flour

50 g (2 oz) butter

50 g (2 oz) grated Parmesan cheese

50 g (2 oz) grated Cheshire or similar cheese

pinch cayenne pepper

Hazelnut Honey Biscuits

This is a delicious little cake-like biscuit made with two traditional foods used in Irish cooking, hazelnuts and honey.

Put the shelled hazelnuts on a baking tray in a preheated oven at 190°C/375°F/gas mark 5 for about 10 minutes. When cool enough to handle, rub the skins off and put the nuts through a mill, or blend them using a mini-blender. Sift the flour and salt together. Cream the butter and sugar until light, and add the nuts and the flour mixture, then mix until well blended. Knead lightly, cover and leave for 30 minutes.

Roll out on a lightly floured surface and cut into 5 cm (2 in) rounds. Line a baking tray with rice or parchment paper and put the rounds on. Bake at 190°C/375°F/gas mark 5 for 7–10 minutes, not longer, or the nuts will have a bitter taste. Take from the oven before the biscuits colour. Sandwich together in pairs with a little thick honey between and the icing sugar sprinkled on top.

MAKES ABOUT 12 'SANDWICHES'

75 g (3 oz) shelled hazelnuts
150 g (5 oz) flour
pinch salt
110 g (4 oz) butter
5 rounded tablespoons fine sugar
3–4 tablespoons thick honey
a little icing sugar

Oatmeal and Cinnamon Biscuits

110 g (4 oz) butter

110 g (4 oz) brown sugar

2 eggs, beaten

110 g (4 oz) flour

110 g (4 oz) oatmeal

1 level teaspoon ground cinnamon

½ level teaspoon baking powder

pinch salt

a very little milk if necessary

Cream the butter and sugar, then add the beaten eggs, little by little, adding a little of the flour after each addition. Add the oatmeal, cinnamon, baking powder and salt, and mix well. Add a very little milk if the mixture seems too stiff; it should be a fairly soft dough. Drop spoonfuls onto a greased baking tray and bake at 190°C/375°F/gas mark 5 for 15 minutes. Cool on a rack.

MAKES ABOUT 25 BISCUITS

Honey Scones

Sift the white flour, baking powder and salt together, then add the wholemeal flour and rub in the butter. Stir in the sugar. Add the honey to the milk and stir until dissolved, then add most of the mixture to the flour and butter mixture, and mix to make a soft dough, reserving the rest for a glaze. Shape the dough into a round about 20 or 22 cm (8 or 9 in) across and put onto a greased baking sheet. Cut across the top four times to mark 8 wedge-like portions or farls and bake at 200°C/400°F/gas mark 6 for 20 minutes. Take out to brush with glaze, then put back and continue cooking for 5–10 minutes.

MAKES 8 'FARLS'

110 g (4 oz) white flour
2 level teaspoons baking powder
pinch salt
110 g (4 oz) wholemeal flour
3 tablespoons butter
1 heaped tablespoon brown sugar
1 generous tablespoon honey
150 ml (¼ pint) milk

Tea Brack

450 g (1 lb) sultanas
450 g (1 lb) raisins
450 g (1 lb) brown sugar
3 cups black tea
450 g (1 lb) flour
3 eggs, beaten
3 level teaspoons baking powder
3 level teaspoons mixed spice
warmed honey to glaze

Breac means speckled, i.e. with the fruit. There are two versions of this traditional cake eaten at Hallowe'en. One is yeasted and the other is made with baking powder. This is the version made with baking powder.

Soak the fruit and sugar in the tea overnight.

The next day mix the flour, baking powder and mixed spice, and add alternately the flour mixture and eggs to the soaked mixture.

Turn into three 20 cm (8 in) tins and bake for 1 ½ hours at 160°C/325°F/gas mark 3. Then take out and brush the tops with warmed honey to glaze. Put back for a few minutes to dry. Cool on a wire rack.

SERVES 10–12

Almond Cake

175 g (6 oz) butter
175 g (6 oz) fine sugar
3 eggs
130 g (4 ½ oz) flour, sifted
½ teaspoon baking powder
75 g (3 oz) ground almonds
few drops of almond essence

ICING
175 g (6 oz) icing sugar
1 heaped tablespoon butter
2 tablespoons milk
½ teaspoon almond essence
split blanched almonds

This is a light cake usually made in a 17.5 cm (7 in) square or oblong shallow tin. It is usually iced afterwards.

Cream the butter and sugar together until light. Then add the eggs separately, beating each one in well. Sift the flour and baking powder together and fold into the mixture, then add the ground almonds and the essence.

Line a baking tin with buttered paper and put in the mixture. Bake at 200°C/400°F/gas mark 6 for 20–25 minutes until a skewer inserted in the cake comes out clean. Remove from the oven and leave to cool in the tin for about 5 minutes before completely cooling on a wire rack.

To make the icing, sift the icing sugar into a bowl. Put the butter in small pieces in a saucepan with the milk and almond essence. Stir over a low heat until the butter has just melted, then pour at once into the middle of the icing sugar and beat gently until thick and smooth. (Add a tablespoon of boiling water if the icing is too thick.) Pour quickly over the top of the cake and sprinkle the top with split blanched almonds.

SERVES 8–10

Madeira Cake

This is the cake that was much enjoyed with a glass of Madeira wine. It is a delicious cake, very pure and delicate tasting.

Sift the two flours together twice onto greaseproof paper. Cream together the butter, sugar and grated lemon rind until light. Add the eggs, one at a time, alternately with spoonfuls of the sifted flour, beating in each addition well. Then fold in the remaining flour, using a metal spoon. Add the milk and combine until it makes a fairly soft mixture. Pour into a greased and lined deep 25 cm (10 in) cake tin and bake in the middle of a preheated oven at 160°C/325°F/gas mark 3 for about 45 minutes or until golden in colour. Lay the slice of candied citron peel gently on top of the cake after the first half hour and close the oven door quickly. Test before taking from the oven and leave in the tin for half an hour, then turn out to cool on a wire rack. After it has cooled, take off the paper. To keep, wrap in greaseproof paper and store in an airtight tin in a cool place.

SERVES 8–10

425 g (15 oz) flour

3 heaped tablespoons self-raising flour

350 g (12 oz) butter

225 g (8 oz) sugar

grated rind of 1 lemon

6 large eggs

150 ml (¼ pint) milk

1 thin slice candied citron peel

Gur Cake

8 slices stale bread, crusts cut off

3 tablespoons flour

½ teaspoon baking powder

2 teaspoons mixed spice

110 g (4 oz) brown sugar

2 tablespoons butter

175 g (6 oz) currants or mixed dried fruit

1 large egg, beaten

4 tablespoons milk

350 g (12 oz) shortcrust pastry (see page 260)

sugar for sprinkling

This cake was eaten by the poor of Dublin in the nineteenth and early twentieth centuries, for it was very cheap because it was made by bakers from their stale cake or bread stocks. This can be made with stale cake rather than bread if preferred, in which case omit the dried fruit.

Soak the bread in a little water for an hour, then squeeze the moisture out. Combine the flour, baking powder, mixed spice, sugar, butter, fruit, beaten egg and milk. Mix well.

Line the bottom of a 22 cm (9 in) square tin with half of the pastry and spread the mixture over, then cover with the remaining pastry. Make a few diagonal gashes across the top and bake at 190°C/375°F/gas mark 5 for about an hour. Sprinkle the top with sugar and allow to cool in the tin, then cut into 24 small squares. (A square of this size used to be sold for a halfpenny.)

MAKES 24 'SMALL SQUARES'

Irish Whiskey Cake

peel of 1 large lemon
1 double measure Irish whiskey
175 g (6 oz) butter
175 g (6 oz) fine sugar
175 g (6 oz) flour, sifted
3 eggs, separated
175 g (6 oz) sultanas
pinch salt
1 teaspoon baking powder

To get the true flavour, this lovely cake should be started the evening before.

Put the lemon peel into a glass, cover with whiskey and leave overnight. Cream the butter and sugar until light. Add the egg yolks one at a time, along with a spoonful of flour, mixing well. Add the whiskey through a strainer and mix in the sultanas with a little more flour. Whisk the egg whites stiffly and fold into the mixture with the salt, baking powder and the remaining flour.

Pour into a greased and lined 17.5 cm (7 in) cake tin and bake in a preheated oven at 180°C/350°F/gas mark 4 for 1 ¼–1 ½ hours; test before removing from the oven.

SERVES 8–10

Coconut Cakes

Cream the butter and sugar. Sift the flour with the salt and gradually add to the butter and sugar mixture, stirring all the time. Gradually add the coconut and then the beaten eggs, mixing very well. Drop small spoonfuls onto a greased baking sheet and bake at 220°C/450°F/gas mark 7 for 10 minutes.

MAKES ABOUT 10 CAKES

225 g (8 oz) butter

225 g (8 oz) fine sugar

275 g (10 oz) flour

pinch salt

175 g (6 oz) desiccated coconut

2 large eggs

Cherry Cake

175–225 g (6–8 oz) glacé cherries
175 g (6 oz) butter
175 g (6 oz) sugar
few drops of almond or vanilla essence
3 medium-sized eggs, beaten
275 g (10 oz) self-raising flour
pinch salt

Cherries are popular in cakes in Ireland. They are sometimes added to a sweetened dough mix – this is called 'cherry log'.

Grease and line a 900 g (2 lb) loaf tin with greaseproof paper. Cut the cherries in half, then wash in warm water and dry thoroughly. Cream the butter and sugar, add the essence and the beaten eggs, little by little, beating well after each addition. Fold in the sifted flour, salt and cherries. Put into the tin and bake at 190°C/375°F/gas mark 5 for 1 ½ hours or until a skewer inserted comes out clean. Cool on a wire rack.

MAKES 900 G (2 LB)

Melting Moments

These very light, little cakes of Scottish origin (but now firmly established in Ireland) live up to their name.

Cream the butter and sugar until very light. Add both flours gradually, mixing well. Put small spoonfuls onto greased baking trays and bake for about 15 minutes in the oven at 180°C/350°F/gas mark 4. Cool on a rack, and when cool, sandwich together with a little lemon curd or thick honey in between.

MAKES ABOUT 30 'SANDWICHES'

275 g (10 oz) butter
50 g (2 oz) icing sugar
225 g (8 oz) sifted flour
50 g (2 oz) cornflour
lemon curd or thick honey

Ginger Cup Cakes

Combine the ingredients, adding just enough fruit juice to form a nice dough, and bake in greased cup-cake tins at 190°C/375°F/gas mark 5 for 15 minutes.

MAKES ABOUT 16 CUP CAKES

225 g (8 oz) flour
½ teaspoon baking powder
½ teaspoon ground ginger
½ teaspoon mixed spice
3 heaped tablespoons butter
3 heaped tablespoons sugar
1 tablespoon golden syrup
a little fruit juice

Black Forest Cake

6 large eggs

150 g (5 oz) castor sugar

50 g (2 oz) sifted cocoa powder

25 g (1 oz) sifted self-raising flour

300 ml (½ pint) double cream, whipped

1 level tablespoon castor sugar

1 × 450 g (1 lb) tin black cherries, stoned

50 g (2 oz) dark chocolate

1 tablespoon rum or kirsch

fresh cherries to decorate

Oil two 20 cm (8 in) sandwich tins and line the base with oiled greaseproof paper. Separate the eggs: yolks in one bowl, whites in a larger one. Whisk the yolks with the 150 g (5 oz) sugar until pale and thickened slightly, then fold in the cocoa and sifted flour. With a clean whisk, beat the whites until stiff but not dry. Stir a heaped tablespoon of egg white into the cocoa mixture, then gently fold in the rest using a metal spoon. (Do it very gently.) Divide this mixture between the tins and bake near the centre in a preheated oven at 180°C/350°F/gas mark 4 for about 15–20 minutes.

They may not appear fully cooked but should be set and slightly puffy. They will shrink quite a lot, which is normal. Leave the cakes to cool in the tins but turn out while still faintly warm and strip off the papers. Now whip the cream with the 1 tablespoon of sugar until floppy but not too stiff. Empty the can of cherries into a sieve over a bowl. Then mix 2 tablespoons of the juice with 1 tablespoon rum or kirsch and sprinkle this over the cake layers.

Using a palette knife, spread about one-third of the whipped cream over one cake. Take any stones from the cherries and arrange the cherries over the cream on the cake. Put onto a serving dish. Carefully lift up the other layer and put on top. Cover the entire cake with the rest of the cream using a palette knife. Arrange the fresh cherries around the edges, or make a pattern, and finally grate the chocolate over the top and sides of the cake. Do not move the cake from the surface it is on and keep covered loosely with paper in a cold place.

SERVES 8

Date and Walnut Cake

This is delicious and one of my favourites.

Preheat the oven to 180°C/350°F/gas mark 4, and lightly oil and line a 900 g (2 lb) loaf tin. Put the chopped dates and milk in a pan and bring to the boil. Leave aside to cool, then drain the dates, but reserve the liquid. Blend half the dates, butter, oil, eggs and date milk together until smooth and creamy. Mix the flour, flakemeal and spice together in a bowl, gradually adding the blended ingredients. Fold in the remaining dates and chopped walnuts, then spoon into the tin. Cook in the centre of the oven for about 1 hour.

MAKES 900 G (2 LB)

175 g (6 oz) dates, pitted and chopped

175 ml (6 fl oz) milk

50 g (2 oz) butter, softened

2 large eggs

50 g (2 oz) flakemeal (rolled oats)

4 tablespoons sunflower oil

175 g (6 oz) wholemeal self-raising flour or plain wholemeal plus 2 level teaspoons baking powder

1 teaspoon ground mixed spice

50 g (2 oz) walnuts, chopped

Chocolate Cheesecake

BASE
75 g (3 oz) butter

175 g (6 oz) digestive
biscuits, crushed

FILLING
450 g (1 lb) cottage or curd
cheese

50 g (2 oz) sugar

1 egg

110 g (4 oz) plain chocolate
such as Bournville or Menier

pinch salt

75 g (3 fl oz) soured or sweet
cream, whipped lightly

½ teaspoon vanilla extract

1 tablespoon Tia Maria, Irish
coffee liqueur or rum

Melt the butter in a pan over a low heat, then remove and stir in the biscuit crumbs. Press into a loose-bottomed flan dish about 20 cm (8 in) in diameter.

Melt the chocolate in a bowl standing over hot water. Whisk the egg with the sugar until creamy, then beat in the cheese, melted chocolate, vanilla, salt, liqueur and soured or sweet cream. Beat until smooth, then pour over the biscuit base and bake at 180°C/350°F/gas mark 4 for about 40 minutes. Chill before serving. The top can be decorated with the liqueur-flavoured whipped cream.

SERVES ABOUT 6, DEPENDING ON APPETITES

Jamaica Gingerbread

This is a lovely dark gingerbread using two syrups.

Preheat oven to 150°C/300°F/gas mark 2, and grease and line an 18 cm (7 in) square cake tin. Warm the margarine, treacle and syrup together in a saucepan until the fat melts, then add the milk. Sieve the dry ingredients. Beat the eggs and add to the liquid. Pour all the liquid into the dry ingredients and beat until smooth. Pour into the tin and bake for 1 ¼–1 ½ hours. If liked, about 50 g (2 oz) sultanas can be added.

SERVES 4–6

110 g (4 oz) margarine
175 g (6 oz) black treacle
50 g (2 oz) golden syrup
150 ml (¼ pint) milk
2 eggs
225 g (8 oz) plain flour
50 g (2 oz) castor sugar
1 rounded teaspoon mixed spice
3 rounded teaspoons ginger
1 level teaspoon bicarbonate of soda

Lemon Marshmallow Cake

225 g (8 oz) self-raising flour
pinch salt
175 g (6 oz) butter or margarine
175 g (6 oz) castor sugar
3 eggs
grated rind and juice of 1 lemon
lemon curd for filling

ICING
225 g (8 oz) icing sugar
2–3 tablespoons lemon juice
approx. 225 g (8 oz) split
marshmallows

This is something you can make a few days ahead. It is light and very fresh tasting. It makes an unusual but not inappropriate Easter cake.

Preheat the oven to 180°C/350°F/gas mark 4. Grease and flour two 20 cm (8 in) sponge tins. Cream together the butter and sugar until light. Beat the eggs with 1 tablespoon of lemon juice. Sieve the flour and salt, and add a spoonful each time you add some of the egg to the butter and sugar mixture. Then fold in the remaining flour and mix well, but do not beat too hard. Spoon the mixture between the two tins and bake in the centre of the oven for about 25–30 minutes or until it moves away from the sides of the tins. Then take out and cool.

Meanwhile, cut the marshmallows in half with wet scissors. When the cakes are cooked, cover the top of one with marshmallow halves slightly overlapping. Put back in the oven for a few minutes so that the marshmallows melt just a little. When both sandwiches are cold, put together with a filling of lemon curd, and then when quite cold, ice the cake.

Sift the icing sugar into a basin, add the strained lemon juice and mix into a smooth paste. Put into a saucepan and warm gently over a low heat, beating well until it is of pouring consistency. You might have to add a little water or milk, but make sure it is very little. Do not let it get too hot or the icing will go dull. Pour warm icing over the cake, smooth the sides, then set aside to chill.

SERVES 8

Christmas Cake

450 g (1 lb) plain flour

175 g (6 oz) castor sugar

175 g (6 oz) soft brown sugar

350 g (12 oz) butter or margarine, cooled at room temperature

110 g (4 oz) ground almonds

110 g (4 oz) walnuts or halved blanched almonds

6 eggs, cooled at room temperature

1 teaspoon mixed spice

½ teaspoon each grated nutmeg and salt

450 g (1 lb) sultanas

450 g (1 lb) seedless raisins

225 g (8 oz) currants

225 g (8 oz) glacé cherries

175 g (6 oz) chopped mixed peel (if possible the whole peel)

110 g (4 oz) dried apricots, soaked

6 tablespoons rum, whiskey or brandy

grated rind of 1 orange and 1 lemon

ICING
See page 231 for royal icing.

Christmas is a time for tradition and in many cases tradition means time. You will save yourself a lot of trouble if you start as early as possible to make the cake and pudding, and not only is it sensible from the time point of view, but many of the Christmas foods are much better if kept for about a month before using. In any case the cake will be much easier to ice if it is left in an airtight tin for several weeks after cooking.

Before you start cooking, check that you have all ingredients to hand: read the recipes through before shopping to make certain you have a full list. Note the tin size for the cake and the size of the puddings, and see that you have the correct ones. This recipe is for a 25 cm (10 in) round cake tin, 23 cm (9 in) square cake tin or two 18 cm (7 in) round tins.

The day before, remove the butter and eggs from the fridge to cool at room temperature. Line the cake tin sides and bottom, first with double thickness brown paper, then lightly oiled greaseproof paper. Prepare the fruits by chopping the drained apricots and cherries and blanching and chopping the nuts. Mix all the fruit and nuts together except the ground almonds and put into a large ovenproof dish. Cover with foil and heat in a low oven 110°C/225°F/gas mark ¼ until the fruit is warmed through and plumped up. Mix with a wooden spoon so that the heat is evenly distributed. When sticky, remove from the oven and let it get quite cold.

To make the cake, cream together the butter and sugars until light and fluffy, then add the eggs, separately, with two teaspoons of flour (to prevent curdling), beating well between each addition. Gently but very thoroughly and using a metal or wooden spoon, fold in the remaining flour, spices, ground almonds and salt. Do not beat for it only makes the cake hard.

Stir in the prepared fruit gradually, having first separated them by light stirring. Finally, add 4 tablespoons of the spirits, mixing well through the mixture. Put the mixture into the prepared tin or tins. Wet a spatula or thick knife with water and run over the top to smooth down. (If you find you are quite exhausted by all this, the tins can be left in a cool place overnight and you can start the long baking first thing in the morning.)

Preheat the oven to 175°C/325°F/gas mark 3. Cover the tin or tins with a lid or foil and set on the middle oven rack. After half an hour reduce the heat to 140°C/275°F/gas mark 1 and after 2 hours remove the lid. Continue baking for about 3 more hours, lowering the temperature slightly if browning and baking too fast.

Test before removing from the oven either with a thin skewer or by pressing the centre with the fingers. It should feel firm and there should be no 'singing' noise. If available, pour over 2 more tablespoons of spirits, first pricking the top with a thin skewer. Leave in the tin to get cold, then wrap in double greaseproof paper and brown paper before storing in an airtight tin. If making two smaller cakes, the procedure is the same, but make the cooking time about 4 ½ hours.

MAKES A 25 CM (10 IN) ROUND CAKE TIN, 23 CM (9 IN) SQUARE CAKE TIN OR TWO 18 CM (7 IN) ROUND TINS

Wedding Cake

130–150 guests: 3 tiers – 28 cm (11 in), 23 cm (9 in), and 15 cm (6 in)

115–130 guests: 2 tiers – 28 cm (11 in) and 23 cm (9 in)

95–115 guests: 2 tiers – 28 cm (11 in) and 20 cm (8 in)

55–65 guests: 1 tier – 23 cm (9 in)

40–50 guests: 1 tier – 23 cm (9 in)

25–35 guests: 1 tier – 20 cm (8 in)

These recipes make a three-tier cake which should be made at least a month in advance, wrapped in foil and kept in an airtight tin. To make it even richer you can, during this time, unwrap the foil, turn the cakes upside down, make small holes with a thin skewer and drop small amounts of either brandy or sherry into the holes with a mustard spoon. Unless you are extremely good at it, I would suggest that you have the icing done by a professional, for it must be firm to hold the other cakes. To achieve this, at least 3 layers of icing must be applied with at least 1 day between each one to allow for it to set really firmly.

The first thing to decide is how many guests there are likely to be, so the guide I am giving below can help. If you have a lot of friends and relations living abroad, then I would make an extra tier, keep it aside and use that for sending away only. You will also have to decide whether you want a round or square cake: these ingredients are for round cakes, so put the mixture for a square cake into a tin 2.5 cm (1 in) smaller than the round tin.

FOR A 28 CM (11 IN) CAKE

700 g (1 ½ lb) currants

400 g (14 oz) sultanas

400 g (14 oz) raisins

110 g (4 oz) mixed peel, finely chopped

110 g (4 oz) glacé cherries, rinsed and finely chopped

6 tablespoons brandy, whiskey or sherry

Put all the ingredients above into a bowl the night before, mixed with the alcohol. Cover and leave for at least 12 hours.

The next day, you will need:

450 g (1 lb) plain flour

½ teaspoon grated nutmeg

1 teaspoon mixed spice

1 ½ tablespoons black treacle

grated rind of 2 lemons and 2 oranges

450 g (1 lb) soft brown sugar

450 g (1 lb) butter

8 standard-sized eggs

110 g (4 oz) almonds, blanched and chopped

First prepare the 28 cm (11 in) round tin, or a 25 cm (10 in) square tin, by brushing it with melted butter and then lining the base and sides with greaseproof paper (double for sides). Brush again with butter. Finally, line the base again and brush with butter.

Make certain all ingredients are at room temperature.

Preheat the oven to 140°C/275°F/gas mark 1. Sift the flour and spices into a bowl. In a large mixing bowl, cream the butter and sugar until light and very fluffy. Then beat the eggs and add a tablespoon at a time, beating well after each addition. When all is incorporated, fold in the flour mixture gradually. Then stir in the fruit, nuts and warmed treacle, followed by the orange and lemon rinds.

Spoon into the prepared tin, spreading evenly, then make a small depression in the centre. Do not fill more than 4 cm (1 ½ in) from the top of the tins. Wrap some thick brown paper around the outside, to protect the edges from the heat, and cover the top with a piece of double greaseproof paper with a hole about the size of a 50c piece cut in the centre.

Bake on the lower shelf of the oven for about 5 ½ hours. Do not open the oven door during cooking. Cool on a wire rack.

FOR A 23 CM (9 IN) CAKE

500 g (1 lb 2 oz) currants
250 g (9 oz) raisins
250 g (9 oz) sultanas
60 g (2 ½ oz) mixed peel, finely chopped
60 g (2 ½ oz) glacé cherries, rinsed and chopped
4 tablespoons brandy, whiskey or sherry

Soak all the above ingredients in the alcohol overnight.

The next day, you will need:

275 g (10 oz) plain flour, sifted
½ teaspoon each mixed spice and nutmeg
1 tablespoon black treacle
275 g (10 oz) soft brown sugar
275 g (10 oz) butter

5 standard-sized eggs

75 g (3 oz) almonds, blanched and chopped

grated rind of 1 lemon and 1 orange

Prepare a 23 cm (9 in) cake tin and preheat the oven as for the 28 cm (11 in) cake above. Follow all instructions for the cake above, but cook for 4 ½–4 ¾ hours. Test before taking out and leave a little longer if necessary.

FOR A 15 CM (6 IN) CAKE

225 g (8 oz) currants

75 g (3 oz) raisins

75 g (3 oz) sultanas

50 g (2 oz) each mixed peel and glacé cherries, rinsed and chopped

2–3 tablespoons brandy, whiskey or sherry

Soak all the above ingredients in the alcohol overnight.

The next day, you will need:

110 g (4 oz) plain flour, sifted

pinch each mixed spice and nutmeg

110 g (4 oz) butter

110 g (4 oz) soft brown sugar

grated rind of ½ lemon and ½ orange

25 g (1 oz) ground almonds

25 g (1 oz) almonds, blanched and chopped

3 standard-sized eggs

1 tablespoon black treacle

Prepare a 15 cm (6 in) cake tin and preheat the oven as for the 28 cm (11 in) cake above. Follow all instructions for the cake above, but the cooking time will be about 3 ½ hours, but test before taking the cake out.

Easter Simnel Cake

This cake was originally made for servant girls to take home on Mothering Sunday and it was often kept until Easter. The name comes from 'Siminellus' which was a festive Roman bread eaten during the spring fertility rites. The eleven small marzipan balls put on top are said to represent the apostles, minus Judas Iscariot.

Preheat oven to 150°C/300°F/gas mark 2. Prepare a 20 cm (8 in) cake tin by lining with greaseproof paper and then oiling the paper. Cream the butter, then add the sugar and beat until light and fluffy. In a separate bowl beat the eggs, then add gradually, beating well after each addition. When beaten, use a metal spoon to fold in the fruits, peel and grated rinds. Sift the flour, baking powder and spice, then carefully fold in alternately with the milk using a metal spoon. Do not beat, just fold lightly. Spoon half the mixture into the cake tin.

Then make the almond paste by mixing all the ingredients in the order given. Roll out just under half and put on top of the cake mixture, then put the rest of the cake mixture on top and level out. Bake in the centre of the oven for 2 ½–3 hours. Leave to cool for 15 minutes before turning out on a rack. When cool, brush with the jam and cover with the paste; roll the remainder of the paste into eleven little balls and place these around the outer edge of the top. Brush with egg and grill until a toasted golden-brown colour. It keeps well in a tin.

SERVES ABOUT 8–10

175 g (6 oz) butter
175 g (6 oz) sugar
3 large eggs, beaten
175 g (6 oz) sultanas
175 g (6 oz) currants
50 g (2 oz) chopped candied peel
1 teaspoon mixed spice
grated rinds of 1 small orange and lemon
225 g (8 oz) plain flour
1 level teaspoon baking powder
3 tablespoons milk, brandy or rum

TOPPING AND FILLING
350 g (12 oz) ground almonds
350 g (12 oz) icing sugar, sieved
3 egg yolks
2 teaspoons lemon juice
few drops almond essence
approx. 1 tablespoon sherry
(almond paste, commercial can be used, about 4 packets)

GLAZING
2 teaspoons apricot jam
1 small egg, beaten

Upside Down Cake

4 tablespoons golden syrup

150 g (5 oz) self-raising flour

75 g (3 oz) butter

2 tablespoons milk

enough fruit to cover the bottom of the dish

1 egg

2 tablespoons sugar

small pinch salt

Upside Down Cake is a name that amuses children and is also very good. It can be made with fresh or tinned fruit and is best eaten cold. Use a round ovenproof dish about 20 cm (8 in) across.

If using raw fruit, cook it in the syrup for about 15 minutes before adding the sponge. Preheat the oven to 180°C/350°F/gas mark 4, put the syrup in the bottom of the dish and arrange the fruit so that it completely covers in overlapping slices. Heat in the oven until the syrup is bubbling and the fruit soft if using raw. Meanwhile, cream the butter and sugar, add the egg and then the salt and flour gradually, stirring well until blended. If it seems too stiff, add the milk. Spread this mixture evenly over the hot fruit and syrup, and cook in the oven for about 20–30 minutes until a skewer comes out clean. (If this seems like too much trouble, use a packet of sponge mixture and proceed as above.) When cool, run a knife round the edges, put a larger plate on top and tip over so that the fruit is on top.

SERVES 6–8

Icings

COFFEE ICING

Sift 225 g (8 oz) icing sugar into a saucepan. Add 2 teaspoons of coffee essence or strong black coffee and about 150 ml (¼ pint) warm water. Stir well over a low heat to dissolve the sugar. It is ready when thick enough to coat the back of a wooden spoon.

AMERICAN ICING

Beat 2 egg whites in a bowl until starting to stiffen. Put 225 g (8 oz) of granulated sugar with 150 ml (¼ pint) water in a saucepan and bring to the boil – boil until it reaches 120°C/250°F. Quickly pour the liquid syrup into the bowl with the egg whites and beat until the mixture begins to thicken. Ice the cake immediately.

ALMOND PASTE

The following amount will cover the top of the cake only which is usual. If the sides are to be spread, double the quantities.

400 g (14 oz) ground almonds
200 g (7 oz) icing sugar or more if necessary
200 g (7 oz) fine sugar
½ teaspoon almond essence
juice of 1 lemon
1 large egg or 3 egg yolks
a little apricot jam, warmed

Mix the ground almonds and both sugars well, and make a well in the centre. Beat the egg, add the lemon juice and almond essence, and pour into the well in the sugar and almond mixture. Gently blend all together with the fingers, for over-kneading will make the almonds oily. (The paste should be pliable but not sticky.) Add more lemon juice or icing sugar if necessary. Dust a board with icing sugar and roll out the paste to the size of the cake top.

If the top of the cake is not straight, cut to make the surface level, then turn the cake over so that the flat bottom becomes the top. Press the warm apricot jam through a sieve and brush onto the top of the cake. Gently reverse the cake again to lay the apricot side down onto the round of almond paste. Press down lightly and trim round the edges. Put the cake board or plate over it and invert. Cover lightly with tissue paper and leave to harden for a week. It will then be ready for royal icing if using.

This is the icing used on Christmas cakes or other rich cakes for special occasions, which are first covered with the almond paste (see above). The almond paste is put on at least a week before the royal icing to dry thoroughly. The icing itself should be made two or three days before the cake is to be eaten. If a thick double icing is wanted, the first coat should be left to dry for 24 hours before applying the second coat. The cake should be on the plate or cake board from which it will be served, and when finished, the whole cake should be covered loosely with tissue paper, not put into a tin or it will 'sweat' and be spoiled. The following ingredients are enough for the top and sides of a 25 cm (10 in) round cake.

ROYAL ICING

Sift the icing sugar twice. Put the egg whites in a bowl and stir lightly with a fork, but do not beat. Add most of the sifted sugar a little at a time, beating well with a wooden spoon between each addition. Add the lemon juice, glycerine and remaining sugar, beating very well to get rid of any tiny air bubbles and until the icing becomes really smooth. Cover with a dampened cloth until ready to apply.

900 g (2 lb) icing sugar
1 teaspoon lemon juice
4 egg whites
2 teaspoons glycerine

If necessary, cut the top of the cake to make the surface level, then turn over so that the flat bottom is the top. The icing should be smoothed over the entire cake, top and sides, using a plastic ruler or icing knife, and left to dry naturally.

PRESERVES, CHUTNEYS AND JAMS

'Chutneys can cheer up the simplest
meal, from bread and cheese to a
dollop in a casserole or mixed into a
minced beef mixture.'

Tomato Chutney

1.4 kg (3 lb) tomatoes, chopped

450 g (1 lb) onions, finely chopped

1 heart of celery, finely chopped, or 2 lovage leaves, finely chopped

300 ml (½ pint) white vinegar

1 teaspoon each salt and cayenne pepper

2–3 medium-sized cooking apples, peeled and roughly chopped

3 tablespoons sultanas

225 g (8 oz) brown or white sugar

pinch each ginger, mace, cinnamon and nutmeg

A perennial favourite which tastes so good and can be used for many things. A spoonful or so in a casserole dish can add a piquant flavour and a little added to a Welsh rarebit type of dish before grilling is very good. My recipe is old and very adaptable. In fact, one time I made some, the cayenne pepper came out in rather a rush and I thought I had put too much in. However, it gave a slightly warm taste which we found pleasant. I am always undecided as to whether to peel the tomatoes or not: the skins do add something and it is quite easy to hook out the biggest pieces before bottling, but if you really dislike skins, then plunge the tomatoes in boiling water and skin before using them.

Put the tomatoes and the other vegetables into a saucepan with the vinegar. Add the apples, spices, salt and pepper, bring to the boil and simmer fairly hard for about 2 hours. After 1 ½ hours, add the sultanas and sugar, dissolving well. Boil until reduced, then put in warmed jars and cover when cold. If it is still too liquid (owing to the tomatoes being overripe), then thicken with 1 tablespoon cornflour creamed in water. Green tomatoes can also be used, but add a little more sugar.

MAKES ABOUT 2 KG (4 LB)

Apple Chutney

1.4 kg (3 lb) apples

2 large onions

1 litre (1 ½ pints) white vinegar

900 g (2 lb) brown sugar

½ teaspoon cayenne pepper

2 teaspoons salt

350 g (12 oz) raisins

110 g (4 oz) ginger, chopped, optional

1 level teaspoon dry mustard

Probably the cheapest to make, especially if you have a few trees in the garden.

Peel, core and chop the apples and onions, and put into a saucepan. Add the vinegar and boil gently for about 20 minutes, then add all the other ingredients, mixing well. Bring to the boil, then simmer for about 30–45 minutes, stirring from time to time so that it does not stick. When it is fairly dark and thick, take off and put into warmed jars.

MAKES ABOUT 2.3 KG (5 LB) CHUTNEY

VARIATION: It is extremely good if instead of the raisins, 450 g (1 lb) chopped cooking dates are added and a pinch of ground cloves or mixed spice.

Plum or Pear Chutney

Another delicious and unusual chutney, very good with pork and chicken.

Cook the fruit and vegetables with the vinegar until softened, then add all the other ingredients and simmer for 1–1 ½ hours. Bottle as usual.

MAKES ABOUT 2 KG (4 LB)

1.4 kg (3 lb) stoned plums or peeled and cored pears

450 g (1 lb) minced carrots

450 g (1 lb) raisins or sultanas

450 g (1 lb) soft brown sugar

600 ml (1 pint) white vinegar

25 g (1 oz) garlic

2 teaspoons ginger

35 g (1 ½ oz) salt

Dundee Marmalade

Wash the oranges well and pick off any stalks, then put into a large saucepan with 1.7 litres (3 pints) water. Cover and bring to the boil, then simmer gently for about 1 hour or until the peel is quite soft, enough to be able to squeeze it between the fingers. Lift out the oranges with a slotted spoon (you can do a few at a time if you like), put onto a large meat dish and cut in half.

Have a small saucepan by you. With a spoon, scoop out the pips and pith from the middle, put into the small saucepan and pile the half-shells up into groups of about four. Do this until they are all done, then cover the pith and pips with the remaining water. Squeeze out the juice from the lemons and add to the large saucepan of liquid the oranges were boiled in. Add the lemon peels to the pips and pith. Boil this latter small saucepan up, then simmer for about 15 minutes to remove all pectin and strain into the large saucepan.

With a sharp knife, cut up the groups of four half-shells into the thickness you like the peel to be, then add to the big saucepan along with the sugar.

Now comes the important point: once the sugar is added, it must be stirred over a moderate heat until it is quite dissolved, before boiling up for a set. Any remaining crystals left in will cause crystallisation when the marmalade is stored. Once dissolved, boil rapidly for about 15–20 minutes and test by putting a little on an iced saucer to see if it crinkles, or use a sugar thermometer – it is ready when it reaches 108°C/220°F.

Take the pan off the heat when setting point is reached. Cool for 10–15 minutes before potting, as this ensures that the peel is evenly distributed. Cover with waxed paper or a good screw-top lid.

MAKES ABOUT 3.6 KG (8 LB)

1.4 kg (3 lb) Seville oranges
2 litres (3 ½ pints) water
juice of 2 lemons
2.7 kg (6 lb) sugar

Bramble Jelly

This is made by boiling the blackberries with 2 apples to every 450 g (1 lb) of berries, barely covered with water, for half an hour. Drain well or drip overnight. Then measure the juice and add 450 g (1 lb) sugar for every 600 ml (1 pint) juice and, after dissolving the sugar, boil hard for 15 minutes.

Strawberry Jam

3.2 kg (7 lb) strawberries
6 tablespoons lemon juice
3.2 kg (7 lb) sugar

Use only unripe strawberries.

Prepare the fruit and put into the pan with the lemon juice, then leave for a few hours to draw out the juice. Put over a low heat until the juices all come out and continue to simmer, stirring well, until the fruit is soft. Add the sugar, stir until dissolved over a low heat, then boil rapidly for about 15 minutes. Let it cool for 10 minutes so that the fruit is evenly distributed when you bottle it. Securely cover at once.

MAKES APPROXIMATELY 5.4 KG (12 LB) JAM

Raspberry Jam

Prepare the fruit and put into a large saucepan with the lemon juice, squashing a little at the bottom to assist in the juice coming out, but leave some whole. Simmer for about 5 minutes, add the sugar, stirring all the time until it is dissolved. Then boil up rapidly for about 12–15 minutes.

2.7 kg (6 lb) raspberries
2.7 kg (6 lb) sugar
2 tablespoons lemon juice

MAKES APPROXIMATELY 5.4 KG (12 LB)

Plum Jam

Use the same amount of sugar as fruit, and for 2.3 kg (5 lb) fruit, add 300 ml (½ pint) water and the juice of ½ a lemon, about 2 teaspoons. Cook this for about 20 minutes until the fruit is soft, then add the sugar and stir until dissolved. Then increase the heat and boil rapidly for about 10–15 minutes.

You can stone the fruit before cooking, or skim off the stones as they rise to the surface, but in the latter case I have noticed that a few do slip by.

MAKES ABOUT 4.5 KG (10 LB) JAM

VARIATION: A little apple can be added if liked.

Blueberry Jam

I like to make a few pounds of this lovely jam, which can be used as a topping for cheesecakes or tarts as well. Blueberries do not have a lot of pectin, so it is wise to use added pectin for a perfect set.

For 900 g (2 lb) fruit (which needs no picking over), use 300 ml (½ pint) water and let cook for about 15 minutes. Then add 900 g (2 lb) sugar and dissolve slowly before adding the juice of 1 lemon and boiling up quickly for about 10 minutes. Finally, add a bottle of Certo, stirred well, and then bottle.

MAKES ABOUT 1.8 KG (4 LB) JAM

Tutti-frutti

450 g (1 lb) prepared
rhubarb, chopped

3 oranges

This is a superb jam recipe given to me by Eileen Lawlor of
Ballyshannon, Co. Donegal. It belonged to her grandmother,
Violet Stopford Lawlor and is at least one hundred years old.
The Lawlor family often serve it sandwiched between a very
light sponge cake.

If possible, peel the whole rind from the orange, then squeeze
out the juice. Pour over the rhubarb and leave overnight.

Then take:

225 g (8 oz) dried apricots
225 g (8 oz) prunes
110 g (4 oz) dried figs
juice and rind of 1 large juicy lemon

Soak the fruit in the lemon juice, whole lemon rind and
whole orange rind (from above), made up with enough water
to cover, and leave overnight.

The next day take:

3 large apples, peeled, cored and sliced
2 cloves
50 g (2 oz) whole almonds, chopped

Add this to either fruit mixture and leave overnight.

Then mix all together, having removed any stones from the
prunes and taken out the fruit rinds. Bring to the boil and
simmer for about 20 minutes. To every cup of pulp or liquid,
add 1 cup sugar. Dissolve slowly over low heat stirring all
the time, then boil for about 20–30 minutes until, as Eileen
Lawlor says, it is dark and delicious.

Picnic or Packed Lunch

By Theodora FitzGibbon

PACKED LUNCHES can be an awful headache day after day, and somehow it is more difficult to think of changes in the summer, when almost anything goes down well in the cold, dark days of winter! Also in warm weather one doesn't want to eat too much carbohydrate, which is both fattening and over-heating, and after all, sandwiches are at least two-thirds bread and not very exciting. If you are the racehorse type who never puts on weight, then I suggest some of the fruit and nut protein loaves which are a cross between bread and a cake, filling, and not over-fattening. Also they have a great deal more flavour than the usual bread available.

All the following ideas are perfect for either a picnic or for having your lunch alfresco in a park, or some other open space, where you will at least get some sun and fresh air if confined to an office for most of the day.

There are several ways of avoiding too much bread and the simplest to fill one or two of those margarine tubs (which have tight lids) with a good cooked and raw salad; use things like leftover peas, beans, or young carrots, mixed with either freshly shredded cabbage, celery, a little onion if you like it, radishes, strips of green pepper, in fact whatever is available. Then mix through it either cooked, boned and flaked fish (smoked mackerel is excellent, or tuna or sardines, both drained); or chopped ham, bacon, grated cheese, chicken, or any leftover meats. To this can be added a little cold, cooked rice, or those little cooked pasta shapes if you want to make it more substantial, and over the top put some fresh mayonnaise, or a good squeeze of lemon and plain yoghurt if weight is a problem. See photograph for peas. This is delicious eaten with some Energen crispbread, and they now make them in many different flavourings, or those crunchy little triangles of puff, they call Terns. If you don't have to worry about weight then take a few crisp, fresh rolls to have with the salads.

SAVOURY ROLLS are another idea with a minimum of calories and maximum of taste. Blend together about ¼lb cottage or cream cheese with a little salt, cayenne and about 2 oz or several rounds of drained cucumber, or tinned pineapple. Add a little chopped ham and a few fresh herbs, then put into the little tubs and serve with crispbread. Or omit the ham

COTTAGE CHEESE also has the advantage in that it can be used for a sweet or savoury, so if you're passionately addicted to sweet things, yet feel guilty about it, then use cottage cheese mixed with a little honey or sugar to taste, and add chopped fruits and a few nuts to the mixture. This makes an excellently, fresh last course, and again can be served from those little tubs. Yoghurt is of course another idea and there are now so many flavours, that everyone should be satisfied. Or simply settle for fresh fruit which is full of vitamins, and in the case of apples, very good for the teeth.

STUFFED EGGS are another good idea, and wedged into those tubs, stand up to travelling very well so long as you don't stand them upside-down. Hard boil as many eggs as are needed for not longer than 10 minutes, then put them under cold running water. This prevents them overcooking and having that unattractive black ring around the yolks. When cold, shell, cut in half across and put the yolks into a bowl. Snip off a tiny bit of the whites so that they stand up. Mix the mashed yolks with salt, pepper, a dash of Worcestershire or tomato purée if you like it, and add a little grated cheese, or mashed sardine, or finely shredded ham, and a few fresh herbs if you have them. Mix it very well and if very stiff add a trickle of yoghurt or a little top of the milk but don't make it sloppy. Put this mixture back into the whites, put into the tubs and wedge the gaps with bits of crisp lettuce, radishes or snippets of green pepper. Two eggs would be a usual helping and very low in calories.

AUSTRALIAN APPLE CHEESE BREAD is full of protein and can be eaten plain or with butter, or used, sliced thinly for a super lettuce sandwich. The following amounts make 16 slices about half-an-inch thick:

8 oz self-raising flour
½ teaspoon salt
4 oz butter or margarine
4 oz caster sugar
2 oz grated Cheddar cheese
1 cup (2 oz) chopped walnuts
2 large Granny Smith apples (for preference) peeled, cored and shredded
2 eggs.

Sift the flour with the salt, then in a separate bowl cream the butter and sugar until light and fluffy. Add the grated cheese and mix well. Beat the eggs and add them little by little with a little flour,

flour and blend again. Put into a buttered loaf tin 8¼" x 5¼" and bake in a moderate oven (375°F, Gas Mark 4) for one hour. Turn out and cool on a wire tray, and let it get quite cold before cutting.

•

APPLE AND CHERRY SPICED LOAF

4 oz butter or margarine
4 oz caster sugar
2 eggs
1 tablespoon honey
4 oz raisins or sultanas
2 oz. glacé cherries
8 oz self-raising flour
1 large apple, peeled, cored and chopped
pinch of salt.
1 level teaspoon mixed spice

Cream the butter and sugar, then add all the other ingredients adding a little flour each time some egg is mixed through. Beat very well for about two minutes. Turn into a greased two-pound loaf tin and bake at 350°F (Gas Mark 4) for one hour. Reduce the heat to Mark 3 (325°F) for a further 15-20 minutes. Turn out and cool on a wire tray and leave to get quite cold before slicing. Makes about the same as above loaf.

For A Rainy Cold Evening

DEVILLED STEAK AND KIDNEY CASSEROLE PIE

1½ lb. braising steak
½ lb. ox kidney
1 large onion
2 large carrots
2 tablespoons oil
One 10½ oz. can condensed tomato and rice soup
½ pint beef stock or water
1 level teaspoon curry powder
½-1 teaspoon crushed dried chilli pepper
1 bayleaf

Cut the steak and kidney into one-inch cubes. Peel and slice the onion and carrot. Heat the oil and sauté the meat and vegetables for 5-10 minutes. Add the remaining ingredients, cover and simmer for about 1-1½ hours or until the meat is tender. Add a little more stock or water during cooking if necessary. Serve with baked potatoes and green vegetables or alternately

BASIC RECIPES

'Sauce comes from the Latin *salsus*, the word for salted: the word *saucer* comes from *sauce*, for in Norman times sauce was poured into individual saucers and each person dipped his food, according to his taste, into the sauce.'

Brandy Butter

225 g (8 oz) butter
75–110 g (3–4 oz) castor sugar
4 tablespoons brandy

Cream the butter until quite light and soft, then gradually beat in the castor sugar, seeing that it is well absorbed each time. Gradually add the brandy, beating each time, so that the brandy does not curdle the butter. Put into the pot, cover and keep cool. This will keep well in a screw-top jar in the fridge.

FOR ABOUT 10 PEOPLE

Cranberry Sauce

450 g (1 lb) cranberries

juice and grated rind of 1 orange

110 g (4 oz) sugar (or substitute)

about 4 tablespoons water

a little brandy

Take the cranberries and put into a saucepan with the juice and rind of the orange, sugar (or substitute) and water. Bring to the boil and then simmer until just soft. Take off and taste for sweetness, but do not make too sweet; this sauce should be a foil for the rich food. Cool, then put into an airtight screw-top jar and float a little brandy over the top before closing. Keep in a cool place until needed. It will keep a year in the fridge and is also good with pork. Although cranberries freeze well, they can seldom be bought except around Christmas time.

FOR ABOUT 10 PEOPLE

Cherry Sauce

This is delicious with tongue or duck but can be a little expensive to make. However, black cherry jam can be used instead.

Put all the ingredients into a saucepan and bring to the boil. Simmer for about half an hour or until the sauce is reduced and is a bit syrupy. Serve with hot tongue.

SERVES 4

VARIATION: Use cooked, soaked apricots, chopped, and white wine or cider. This sauce can be made ahead of time and liquidised if liked, then reheated. It is also very good served with cold tongue or ham.

1 tablespoon redcurrant jelly

300 ml (½ pint) red wine

juice of 2 oranges and grated peel of 1

4 tablespoons tongue stock (if not too salty)

1 tablespoon mango chutney, chopped

225 g (8 oz) stoned black cherries, plus 2 tablespoons of the juice, or 3 tablespoons black cherry jam

Rich Chocolate Sauce

225 g (8 oz) plain or
bitter chocolate

1 tablespoon very strong
black coffee

1 tablespoon brandy

300 ml (½ pint) double or
single cream

Break up or roughly chop the chocolate. Then put all the
ingredients into a saucepan and stir over a moderate heat until
the chocolate has melted and the sauce is smooth. Serve hot
or cold.

SERVES ABOUT 10

Honeyed Barbecue Sauce

50 g (2 oz) butter
1 large onion, finely chopped
1 garlic clove, crushed
3 tablespoons honey
1 cup pineapple juice
2 tablespoons white wine vinegar
1 cup tomato juice
salt and pepper
4–6 pork chops, chicken joints or equivalent other meats

This is very good for chicken, pork, steaks, lamb or sausages. It can be made ahead of time and the foods marinated in it.

Melt the butter, then sauté the onion and garlic until soft but not coloured. Add all the other ingredients except the meat, then cover and simmer for 5–10 minutes. When cold, pour over the meats to be cooked and leave for 4 hours.

Rub the pork chops or other meat in seasoned flour, put into a roasting tin, then brush a little of the sauce over and cook at 190°C/ 375°F/gas mark 5 for 30 minutes. Cook in the oven for a further 15 minutes, brushing with the sauce during cooking, turning once. Then cook again for a further 5 minutes. Take out the meats, reduce the sauce and serve separately.

SERVES 4–6

VARIATION: If using sausages, they should be fried or grilled to colour before starting. This can also be done over a barbecue.

Super Tomato Sauce

This freezes wonderfully, but keep it for special dishes. The recipe can be doubled without difficulty and canned tomatoes can also be used, but go easy with the juice until you see how the purée develops.

Soften the garlic, onion and bacon in the oil or fat. Add the carrot, chopped tomatoes and wine, breaking down canned tomatoes if using. Raise heat and cook hard, uncovered, for 15 minutes, then slowly for 45 minutes. Add seasonings and sugar, then the oregano after 10 minutes. Put the fresh basil in at the end.

The purée should be chunky and moist but not watery. It is delicious used fresh and excellent later on for sauces (after blending), for tomato soup, for some pasta dishes or for a tomato quiche.

MAKES APPROX. 500 ML (18 FL OZ)

3 large garlic cloves, chopped

1 large onion, chopped

110 g (4 oz) streaky bacon, chopped, optional

2 tablespoons butter or 3 tablespoons oil

1 large carrot, chopped

900 g (2 lb) tomatoes, peeled and chopped

150 ml (5 fl oz) dry red or white wine or sherry

salt, pepper and sugar

dried oregano

fresh basil, chopped

Mayonnaise

2 egg yolks

2 teaspoons tarragon
vinegar or lemon juice

300 ml (½ pint) olive oil

salt and pepper

1 tablespoon boiling water

A whole range of sauces can be made with mayonnaise
as a basis. It is essential to have all ingredients at room
temperature before starting; this can also be made in a food
processor.

Break the egg yolks into a bowl and add half the vinegar.
Add the olive oil, drop by drop, beating all the time until
thick, then let it flow in a gentle stream, beating well. When
the oil is used up, season and add the rest of the vinegar,
mixing well. Finally, add the boiling water, which improves
its keeping properties. If it should curdle (separate), then
break another egg yolk and, drop by drop, add to the curdled
mixture, beating all the time.

MAKES ABOUT 300 ML (½ PINT)

Tartare

This is a well-known sauce served with hot or cold fish. Add
some chopped chives, parsley, chopped capers and chopped
gherkins, with a touch of dijon mustard, to the mayonnaise
(see above) and mix well.

Blender Hollandaise

110 g (4 oz) butter

2 egg yolks

1 teaspoon lemon juice (more
can be added if liked)

salt and pepper

Heat the butter in a saucepan until foaming, then put the egg
yolks into the blender container with the lemon juice, salt and
pepper. Cover and blend for 1 second, then turn off. Take
off the lid and slowly pour the hot butter into the eggs, turn
onto high and then switch off. If the sauce is not needed at
once, pour into a thick saucepan or bowl and stand over tepid
water. Heat up the water before serving and whisk until the
sauce is fluffy and warm. This can be served with poached
salmon, vegetables and eggs.

SERVES 4–6

VARIATION: If 2–3 tablespoons of thick cream or 1 stiffly beaten egg white are
added, it becomes sauce mousseline and is served with fresh asparagus, poached
eggs or fish.

Aioli

A delicious, garlicky Provençal sauce, very good with cold poached or boiled fish or vegetables. It is super served over jacket-baked potatoes instead of butter.

2 garlic cloves
6 tablespoons mayonnaise

Pulp the garlic cloves and add to the mayonnaise. Mix well.

SERVES 3–6

Shortcrust Pastry

225 g (8 oz) flour, sifted

pinch salt (or 2 teaspoons sugar if making sweet pastry)

110 g (4 oz) butter

approx. 4 tablespoons of iced water

For a richer version, an egg can be added to this. It should be added before the water, which will probably need to be only about 2 tablespoons, and should be added very gradually. The choice of salt or sugar will depend on the filling to be used with the crust, whether savoury or sweet.

Sift the flour and add the salt (or sugar). Rub the butter in until the mixture resembles coarse breadcrumbs, then add enough iced water to make a soft but firm dough, about 4 tablespoons. Do not overhandle the dough. Pat the dough into an oval shape on a floured board, then wrap in paper or foil and chill for at last half an hour, longer if possible.

MAKES ENOUGH PASTRY FOR A 20 CM (8 IN) BOTTOM AND TOP CRUST

Flaky Pastry

225 g (8 oz) flour, sifted

½ level teaspoon salt (or sugar if making a sweet pastry)

175 g (6 oz) butter

1 teaspoon lemon juice

iced water to bind

This rich crust is not so generally used in Ireland as shortcrust pastry but is sometimes made when only a top covering is required. The choice of salt or sugar of course depends on the filling it will accompany.

Sift together the flour and the salt (or sugar) into a basin. With a knife mix the fat on a plate until softened, then spread it evenly over the plate and mark into four equal portions. Rub one portion into the flour, add the water and lemon juice, and mix to a dough in the basin.

Turn out onto a lightly floured surface and knead to a smooth dough. Leave to rest for 10 minutes. Then roll out to an oblong shape three times longer than its width. Scatter one third of the remaining butter in small pieces over the upper two thirds of the oblong. Fold the lower third up and over the middle and the top third down over that, and roll out to an oblong again. Rest for 15 minutes. Add another third of the butter and repeat the operation, resting again for 15 minutes, then repeat with the remainder of the butter. Finally, chill for at least half an hour before using.

MAKES ABOUT 225 G (8 OZ)

INDEX

Page numbers set in **bold** indicate photographs